The Expectation of the Poor

The Expectation of the Poor

The Church and the Third World

B. N. Y. VAUGHAN

Bishop of British Honduras

JUDSON PRESS, Valley Forge

DEDICATED

To the Clergy of the Diocese of British Honduras
in appreciation of their loyalty and courage.

THE EXPECTATION OF THE POOR

Copyright © SCM Press Ltd. 1972
First published 1972 by SCM Press Ltd.
Judson Press Edition 1972

Library of Congress Cataloging in Publication Data

Vaughan, Benjamin Noel Young.
    The expectation of the poor.

    Bibliography: p.
    1. Underdeveloped areas. 2. Economic development. 3. Church and
underdeveloped areas. I. Title.
HC59.7.V38   330.9'172'4   72-1993
ISBN O-8170-0571-4

Printed in the U.S.A.

Preface

The purpose of this book is to describe the disillusion which the Third World has felt about development. I hope it will be a contribution, however small, towards a better understanding of the problems of developing countries.

It is also meant to promote better relations between developed and developing countries. I have, therefore, attempted to put the problems in such a way that the issues of development can be considered calmly and without that recrimination which obscures rather than enlightens. Living in this 'global village', in which the greatest danger is division, I am increasingly persuaded that one of the tasks of the church is to open up lines of communication between different interests and so assist that mutual understanding which leads to constructive co-operation. I hope this book may be of some help towards this end.

However, reconciliation which Christians try to promote must keep in mind what the church believes about God, man and the world. For this reason some attempt is made to reflect theologically on development, and the last two chapters are designed to describe the present state of thinking on a theology of development and on man.

The bibliography is compiled to assist further study of the subject.

I am extremely grateful to the Rev. and Mrs Saunders Davies, for their work in making the index. The book would not have been possible, however, without the help of my wife. Thanking her in particular, I wish also to acknowledge my debt to the sources mentioned in the footnotes from which so much material for this book has been derived, but for the interpretation of which I must accept responsibility myself.

Bishopthorpe   BENJAMIN HONDURAS
Belize City
British Honduras, Central America
1st May 1971

Abbreviations

CARIFTA	The Caribbean Free Trade Association
CELAM	Latin American Catholic Episcopal College
CIIR	Catholic Institute for International Relations
EPS	Ecumenical Press Service of the World Council of Churches, Geneva
FAO	Food and Agriculture Organization
IMF	International Monetary Fund
ISAL	Church and Society in Latin America
LAFTA	Latin American Free Trade Association
OECD	Organization for Economic Trade and Development
SDR	Special Drawing Rights (International Monetary Fund)
SODEPAX	Joint Committee on Society, Development and Peace
UN	United Nations
UNCTAD	United Nations Conference on Trade and Development
UNESCO	United Nations Educational, Scientific and Cultural Organization
UNO	United Nations Organization
WCC	World Council of Churches

Bibliographical details not given in the notes will be found in full in the bibliography at the end of the book.

Contents

I

The Development Mirage - Introduction

In an article entitled 'Brazil: An Underdeveloped Giant Wakes Up', Caio de Toledo quotes from the 'Song of the Underdeveloped':

> But one day the giant awoke,
> He ceased being a sleeping giant,
> And lo! a dwarf arose;
> He was an underdeveloped country![1]

This revolutionary song from Brazil tells how people in a developing country in Latin America had been led to expect great things as a result of development. The very word 'development' had glittered with hope for them, as it had for others in the Third World. But when they tried to develop it was found to be an illusion, and the glitter began to wear off.

It was towards the end of the 1960s that the general feeling began to spread in the developing countries that their rising expectations were not going to be realized. The richer nations of the North and West had already become accustomed to disillusion with the promises of development through the technological revolution. In Europe and North America the material gains had for some time appeared to many to be offset by losses in those things which make life human. The spiritual price of these material acquisitions, therefore, was already more than many thoughtful people were willing to pay in the older countries long before the disillusion began for the poorer countries, and a large-scale moral reassessment had already got under way there.

But it was only in the later 1960s that the existing programmes of development began to be widely questioned in the developing countries. People were now asking whether they had committed themselves too easily some years earlier to the Development Decade[2] proclaimed by the United Nations for the 1960s. In 1965, at midpoint in the decade, its progress had been examined by U Thant, the Secretary General of the United Nations. Signs of failure were clearly indicated in his review.[3] He said:

> The misery of much of the developing world is a progressive misery. It threatens to grow worse in the second half of the decade. On the present showing the numbers of unemployed men and women suffering from hunger and malnutrition will be markedly greater in 1970 than today.

Many other signs had been put up that all was not going well with development in the less affluent areas of the world. But it was not until the last years of the decade that the developing countries began to take these signs seriously. It is probably 1968 which brought in the era of realism about development in these countries. Until then they had been dazzled by the splendour of the advanced nations and the opportunity, which release from colonialism into independence offered them, of all the material blessings of the older countries. Aid from the richer countries and trade with them on better terms dictated by independence would bring about a new era. A mirage had been produced by a thirst for a better world in which to live and the promises of this happening. So they struggled to get nearer to the mirage – to find it always receding. In 1968 for many of them it vanished altogether.

That was the year of the United Nations Conference on Trade and Development in New Delhi.[4] At that conference the developing countries asked the richer nations for a more generous share of the world's markets and new economic arrangements which would allow them to catch up on those who had advanced far ahead of them. These concessions were refused, to all intents and purposes. Economic realities as they were seen by the developed nations did not allow them to make concessions which would upset their own trade balances. This refusal was the first and most effective eye-opener to world economic realities that the developing countries had yet been given. It dispelled the mirage of a development through trade concessions just as the mirage of a development through aid had already been dispelled for others some time previously.

The conference called by the Joint Committee of the World Council of Churches and the Roman Catholic Commission on Justice and Peace[5] in Beirut in the same year was designed partly to bring pressures on the developed nations to make these concessions. This in turn had been backed up by the Charter of Algiers where the developing nations published their common cause for the world to see. All these efforts, however, did not avail to produce the trade concessions which the developing countries had by now been convinced were the essential means of achieving healthy economic growth and independence. It was then that the illusion about development as it had been envisaged was effectively dispelled.

The poor countries were now able to discern the signs already put out of the failure of development policies and programmes which had been conceived in the new era of independence. For instance, they were able to realize that the gaps which present programmes were creating between rich and poor indicated that there was something basically wrong with the policy which they had accepted. These gaps had appeared long before this but their meaning had not been understood.

One gap which no one could fail to see, but few discerned, was on the international scene – that between the rich and the poor nations. What U Thant said about it at midpoint only echoed what others had already said, but it had not been heard:

The harsh fact persists that many of the poorest countries have continued to grow most slowly. The growth in developing countries as a whole slowed down from an average annual rate of 4·5% in 1955-1960 to 4% in 1960-1963. At the same time the growth rate in the economically advanced market economies has accelerated from 3·4% in the earlier period to 4·4% in 1960-1963. The gap between the per capita incomes of the developing countries and those of the developed countries has also widened during the 1960s.[6]

The other gap was inside the developing countries themselves, where the few rich were getting richer and the poor were getting poorer and increasing in number.[7] As production techniques were introduced by technology from the West, wealth accumulated in the hands of those westernized groups which had access to the new means of production. The poor who depended on the use of their hands were put out of work and the number of the unemployed and disillusioned increased. It was only when the revolutionary proportions of the gap in the developing countries began to be understood that the development programmes were seriously questioned on a wide scale. It was then that the process began to be analysed and the kind of diagnosis given in the next chapter was given closer attention.

We start in that chapter with the economic scene in the developing world, not only because it is the most important aspect of development, since it deals with the basic needs of life for poor people, but also because it is there that the signs of failure are most evident and are most likely to be taken seriously. I also take it first because in fact the fundamental purpose of development is to provide first of all the material needs of the good life. This means economic change from the older means of production and distribution to the more effective modern methods which have accelerated the rate of growth and consequently the standards of living in the richer nations. It is from the need to make these changes that the other problems dealt with in the succeeding chapters arise and to a significant, though to a lesser extent, have questions arisen about the development programmes of the 1960s.

For instance, economic change causes social change and its healthy direction requires the provision of new structures. A complicated social process is set in motion and the effects of this in the developing countries have been so problematic that people have begun to question the development programme on these grounds also. Let me explain what happens when economic changes are introduced into less developed areas, for example, into a primitive agrarian economy.

Generally speaking agrarian economies are organized around the village and family unit, where each member has a significant place in the agricultural effort on the farm. Whenever industry begins to be diversified from primitive agriculture of this kind the simple social structure begins to change and yields to new formations. Members of the family economic unit, necessary to peasant agriculture, break away. They form new associations and develop the new skills required by the new industries. This may be tourism, a light industry or even the application of technological skills and machinery to production and processing in agriculture itself. Whatever it is, the way of life of the old village is changed. Housewives become waitresses in hotels, girls become typists and secretaries, boys require a skill and fathers find their occupation changed. Instead of the old community of the village with its natural leadership there appear new units of association based on interest or profession or work. New types of leadership are required for trades unions, politics and education.

The changes in social patterns as a result of programmes of industrial development introduced into the less advanced countries have been the subject of innumerable studies. Many of them have been sponsored by the churches.[8] They tend to demonstrate that there are three areas in particular where the effects are problematic: moral, psychological and cultural, so far as these may be distinguished. Ethically, behaviour patterns tend to change as a result of the removal of moral restraints which were exercised in the older close family and village structure.[9] The result is usually an increase in crime and immorality at worst, and the growth of new personal attitudes at best. The psychological effect of change as a result of the removal of the old securities which gave emotional stability in the older social structure, has been a growth of mental diseases and nervous complaints previously not known in these societies. The cultural effects have been a more recent area of study and will be dealt with in the chapter on this subject.

We can divide the changes in these fields into two kinds. There are those changes which inevitably follow from economic development of primitive societies, and there are those changes which are not inevitable but require to be introduced to cope with the situation. Both of these, the inevitable and the required changes, have been found in recent years to be problematic.

Those changes which follow inevitably from economic development have been generally assumed to be the fair price which should be paid for the benefits of an industrial technological society. This is, in fact, the conclusion of the symposium *Cultural Patterns and Technical Change*, edited by Margaret Mead,[10] which was designed to provide direction on the way in which the effects of changes in primitive society, particularly in the field of mental health, should be met. The premise on which this symposium was based was that the inevitable changes produced by economic development must be accepted. But this premise is now being increasingly questioned inside the developing countries themselves. It is being said that these effects are inevitable only if a certain kind of economic development is imposed. They have in mind that kind of change which must be made to accommodate western technology.[11] The effects can be reduced if closer attention is paid to the mechanics of change, particularly to the inbuilt self-interest of western based technological change when it is promoted in non-western countries.

On the other hand, there are the other changes which are required to be introduced in order to cope with those changes which happen inevitably as a result of development. These pose problems of a different kind. Changes which happen inevitably have a strange way of being accepted without great protest or difficulty. The changes required to direct their effects tend to provoke resistance and require human energy, calculation and wisdom to get them accepted. For instance, economic change which produces more wealth is quickly accepted, but the political and social decisions required to cope with expanding wealth are introduced, if at all, with great difficulty. The reallocation of power, fair distribution of the fruits, political change, are issues which have recently raised the questions of revolution and violence, among others. We shall look at these issues in the third chapter.

We come next to politics. Politics is the third area where the developing countries have been disillusioned in their development quest. At the Afro-Asian Conference in Bandung in 1955 the decision was taken to demand political independence first and not to wait for economic viability as a prerequisite to nationhood.

Economic development would follow political independence which would enlist the enthusiasm of the people to develop their own resources. In any case, political freedom was regarded as an end in itself. After Bandung came the era of decolonization and independence. It has been marked by deep questioning about the political context of independence and disillusioned hopes about the democratic processes which would govern it.

The post-independence era of many former colonies and protectorates has been marked in many instances by the rise of dictatorships, one-party democratic systems, oppressive governments and ineffective political party systems. The era has seen *coups* and revolutions which had previously been unknown. This has also led to a disillusion about the political arrangements for development and caused a re-examination to be made of the political necessities of a successful programme. The title of the fourth chapter, 'New Masters, Old Servants', is meant to convey a message about politics which few in the developing countries will miss.

Has the attempt to impose western democracy on non-western societies failed? Does democracy need a different expression in these societies? How can economic development succeed in a society where political decisions are acclimatized to the popular vote and not to economic necessities? These are the questions which are being raised on this issue. Africa has to face the problem whether and at what rate tribalism can yield to national democratic structures. India wrestles with the passage from a religious society to a secular democratic nation through communalism. All the new nations have to face the question whether they should surrender part of their sovereignty to larger wholes in the interests of security and economic efficiency. Old rivalries persist and new claims to political and economic power are made by minorities inside these nations. Is world community the objective to be aimed at immediately or ultimately and what problems does regionalism pose for development and peace? These are some of the questions raised by people disillusioned with the political hopes raised in them fifteen years ago.

While privately among themselves the developing nations are expressing their sense of disappointment about their own political performance, there is no secret about their disillusion with the way in which development programmes have been promoted among them. They say that the development process is planned and initiated from outside and serves the interest of the developed nations which dominate and determine what happens inside the countries over which they have surrendered political control. This is what they call neo-colonialism and they detect it in several forms.

It is discovered in the best intentions of the developed nations. For instance, aid itself is regarded as a form of imposing upon the Third World. The Vietnamese Buddhist leader, Thich Tri Quan, is reported as saying that if the Americans 'cannot find ways of granting aid they will have no place to sell the goods they produce. If they cannot sell the goods the plants will have to shut down. If plants shut down, hundreds of thousands will be out of work. America will then be in danger. That is why we can insult the Americans as much as we please, and they will still do our bidding and grant us aid.' The same review which recorded these words went on to say: 'The influx of the American dollar with the American soldier has tended to make the rich of South East Asia richer, the poor poorer. By the end of 1965 rents in Saigon had risen by as much as 400 per cent.'[12]

One of the arch-critics of American neo-colonialism, Monsignor Ivan Illich, who runs a Documentation Centre in Cuernavaca in Mexico, which is designed to create sensitivity in North Americans to Latin American culture, has recently turned his guns in no uncertain terms on what he calls 'do gooders' who visit Mexico. Addressing a group of students at a conference on Inter-American Student Projects he ended his attack on those who come to Mexico with a mission to impose their culture on poor Mexicans by saying:

I am here to suggest that you voluntarily renounce exercising your power which being an American gives you. I am here to entreat you to freely, consciously and humbly give up the legal right you have to impose your benevolence on Mexico. I am here to challenge you to recognize your inability, your powerlessness and your incapacity to do the 'good' which you intended to do.[13]

However harsh we may think this to be, Illich is expressing what many are now feeling in the developing countries. They feel that their development programmes are imposed upon them from outside to satisfy not their own needs but the needs of those who initiate them. The programmes are projections from their place of origin and not a response to local need. The basic fault, they say, is at the point of initiative and in the places where the original planning is done and the original decisions are taken. Development plans are conceived outside, and not inside, the developing countries which are dominated by decisions taken by those who control the techniques, the finance and the markets. Even the World Council of Churches comes in for criticism. For all its goodwill it still studies these issues from the place where it is located in Geneva, and not in the field itself.

It is for this reason that one of the issues which is being most seriously examined in the field of development policy is the question of initiative and the sources of power which determine the programmes. 'Neo-colonialism' is the popular description of an economic mechanism which many in the developing countries find operating at every level. As we shall see, it is used to describe the transfer of control from external political and military power to economic forces. The neo-colonial idea is that these are manipulated by the richer nations with a view to dominating the poorer developing countries in such a way as to serve the interests of the richer nations. We shall try to assess the neo-colonial accusation and, more important, look for the real factors which pattern economic and other relationships of rich and poor nations.

In the process of development in the poorer countries through modernization, a fifth issue arises. For technology started in the West and has imposed itself on the Third World. This technology is avidly grasped at by the poorer countries as a means of accelerating their production and so of improving standards of living. There is no difficulty in getting technology accepted. But technology demands a completely new culture if the new countries are to assimilate and use it. It transforms the values and assumptions and aims of eastern cultures.

At first the cultural effects of technology were accepted without protest in the developing countries. In recent years, however, dissatisfaction has been expressed at the way in which their culture has suffered. A debate is, therefore, now going on between those who claim that development through technology must gear itself to the indigenous culture and those who insist that local culture must accept the mutations which technology demands. In the sixth chapter on culture we shall look at the issue in greater detail and endeavour to understand the cultural needs of humanity which are in danger of suppression from a purely materialistic conception of development.

The next issue which comes up for reconsideration in the Third World is education. There has been scarcely any doubt in the minds of people in the developing countries that education is good and necessary. They have embraced it eagerly and there is no school anywhere that fails for lack of students. At Uppsala, where the World Council of Churches decided to set up new structures, the one about which the greatest enthusiasm was shown was education. It will make the work now done by the churches much more effective if the World Council of Churches can provide greater assistance in this sector. It is not simply that a great load will be taken off the shoulders of local churches which have been struggling for years to provide this necessary service to the community. But it will mean better provision for that service. For it will be done so much better from an ecumenical base which will have the effect of integrating denominational efforts.

Nevertheless, after the original impetus passed, a great deal of rethinking began in the Third World about education. Its value was not doubted but its goal and form began to raise new questions. Education is one of the most effective conveyors of culture. Its form and content, therefore, are matters about which culturally conscious groups are concerned. So much education originates from the West and these days it is largely structured to prepare people for a technological society, and one with western cultural assumptions built into it. It assumes a class society; it has ideas about wealth, social behaviour and values which are strange to other communities. These assumptions and aims are now being challenged, and so inevitably is the medium of education which conveys them.

So it is that behind the pressures to set up new indigenous universities, not necessarily unrelated to those in other parts of the world, there lies a cultural need and a cultural apprehension in the Third World. Behind the efforts to set up new syllabuses and examination systems inside these countries and regions is an attempt to avoid the setting of standards by external cultural forces. These efforts have other consequences, such as the need to provide textbooks from inside the culture, and not least the problem of translating technological terms into the languages which belong to cultures which are strange to these ideas. The alternative is to let the West spread itself over the Third World. But this is neither good nor is it now likely to happen, as we shall attempt to show in the seventh chapter on education.

The last issue which we shall deal with is one which affects Christians in particular. It is the place of ideologies in development policies and programmes. In many, perhaps even in most developing countries, leaders have found it necessary to provide an emotional incentive which will assist people to adopt attitudes which will promote vigorous involvement in development. Generally this has meant outlining a philosophy designed to give intellectual undergirding to the process. This has produced a number of ideologies which have provided emotional incentives for the people and have been conveyed largely through slogans. On the whole, they have used nationalistic sentiment to promote this.

These ideologies have created problems, particularly for Christians, because they tend to impinge upon areas with which religious belief deals and where ultimate questions are raised. One of the main causes of alarm in this matter is historical. Christians recall the Nazi ideology which effectively engaged the youth of Germany in national effort. But its self-righteousness also produced the greatest horrors experienced by man. There are theological questions which are raised by ideologies also. But it is their practical consequences in development programmes which are the cause for immediate concern, though in fact practical effects are a good theological commentary upon them also. In the eighth chapter we shall look at some of these ideologies and try to assess their validity and value.

To sum up, it is in these ways that the peoples in the developing countries are being disillusioned about their first expectations from the development programme. The gilt has worn off. New reactions are setting in. In some ways they are not unlike those provoked by scientific technology in the advanced countries, where the environmental effects of that form of development are causing new questions to be raised. The poisoned lakes and polluted atmosphere are producing questions about development there also. But they have a character of their own in the Third World and this is coloured by the society where the changes have taken place.

One important type of reaction is that which protests against Christianity itself because it is the religion of the West. For it is the West which has stimulated the changes which have taken place there. This reaction is found particularly in the changeless East. Buddhist and Hindu religious sentiments have been enlisted in the cause of protest in many places in the East, and Christianity has been blamed for the ill-effects without being given credit for any good that may have come.

But it is not only the theological assumptions of Christianity which have been at work in making change possible by changing people's minds. Christian agencies have also had a prominent part in promoting the development process outside the West. The churches themselves, and particularly the World Council of Churches and its Division of Inter-Church Aid, Refugee and World Service, have been deeply involved in Third World development programmes. This is why the churches are being accused of being neo-colonial agencies of western domination through their development programmes.

The church is, therefore, faced with a crisis. This crisis is of two kinds; one is related to the field of its theology and the other to the field of its action. The church is being challenged to produce a theology of development by its experience of development which has largely been brought about by forces released by Christianity itself. The church has to look again at the theological assumptions implicit in its development in the programmes which promote it. The assumptions which caused it to encourage the development process are due for reconsideration in the light of experience. A theology of development is required so that the church's participation in the promotion of change can be directed by theological guidelines which have been thoroughly examined in the light of what has happened in recent years.

Here it is important to realize the part which assumptions play in all human activity. The fact that they are implicit and hidden does not lessen their importance and effectiveness in determining what results from a particular policy or programme. For instance, the assumption that the western type of technological development is good for eastern peoples[14] has been one of the most potent factors in determining the character of change in eastern societies. Yet this assumption has hardly been examined in depth with the deliberate intention of resetting development policy as a consequence. As we proceed we shall find hidden assumptions all along the line, in economic programmes, social policies, cultural changes and politics.

These assumptions, and there are many of them, often have a theological base. In fact, it is their theological character which often lends the tacit assumption its greatest potency in promoting change. The case already cited is an obvious one. Here the theological assumption is that the western interpretation of Christianity is valid outside western culture. But the point is that the Graeco-Roman cultural expression of Christianity in the West is necessarily very different from what it would receive in an oriental culture. This is only one of many hidden assumptions which need to be examined in the process of producing a theology of development.

In fact the most potent catalyst of change – scientific technology – requires us to make some very basic assumptions when we decide to use it to promote development not only in non-western societies but even in the West itself. For we assume that the science on which technology is based is an obedient understanding of creation and not a rationalization of an arrogant human attempt to manipulate nature.[15] This raises the question whether man should listen to nature and obey it, or should impose his will upon it through searching for the places at which it will yield to his designs. There is a nest of theological problems which come to light, as soon as tacit assumptions are questioned. Does the doctrine of man's stewardship over the creation give him a right to manipulate the creation without reference to a higher obedience? If not, what is to determine the uses to which he puts the created order? If, on the other hand, it is claimed that man must obey nature, where does the command to subdue the earth come in?

Questions such as we have just mentioned tend to be resolved into one ultimate question which lies beyond them all. It is the question of man himself. If, as is usually claimed, development is meant for the benefit of man, what do we mean by man? Do we mean that which distinguishes him from the rest of the animal creation, and is it to serve this distinctive part of him that development is to be promoted? If so, what is the distinctively human? Is it possible to distil a formula for humanity which will provide a point of reference for all development programmes?

It is this question mark against man which is the fundamental challenge in the attempt to discover a theology of development. All the issues raised converge on this question; if man is the purpose of development, what is man? The World Council of Churches has found this question to be so crucial that the studies of all its departments and divisions are now being co-ordinated with a view to concentrating on the question of 'the humanum' in an attempt to answer the question – What is man, that development must be mindful of him?

If we can answer this question, 'What is man?' if not positively at least by some negative definition, then we must go on to the other field where the church is challenged. We must examine the action which the church has taken or failed to take in development. We must examine the programmes which it has sponsored, the policies which it has adopted, and the assumptions which are hidden in all it has done, or left undone, in this field of action for development in the Third World. If the involvement of the governments and other agencies of the developed countries in the struggle of the poorer countries to improve their economies and to make the changes necessary for greater material prosperity has been problematic, that of the churches must also raise similar questions since the amount of aid which flows from the churches to the poorer countries exceeds that of all the United Nations agencies together. The kind of question which we need to ask when we come to the final chapter and consider the policy which the church should adopt in action for development will include : What are the effects of its present policies? Do they tend to continue attitudes and relationships of dependence? Do they reflect in a religious form the type of aid which comes from the richer countries? Do they have cultural and social effects which deny the authenticity of the local culture and community? We then have to ask whether the church has any business at all in overseas development or in that of the community where it exists. We must ask what form this should take and get our prescriptions from the theology of development so far as this can be formulated.

NOTES

1. Quoted from *Student World*, No. 1, 1964, by M. M. Thomas in his article, 'Awakened Peoples, Developing Nations and the Dynamics of World Politics' in *Responsible Government in a Revolutionary Age*, ed. Z. K. Matthews, p. 33.

2. See *The United Nations Development Decade – Proposals for Action.*
3. See U Thant, *United Nations Development Decade at Midpoint.*
4. See *United Nations Conference on Trade and Development – Second Session (New Delhi),* Vol. 1. Reports and Appendices.
5. Now called the Joint Committee on Society, Development and Peace (SODEPAX).
6. Op. cit., p. 5.
7. See B. N. Y. Vaughan, *Wealth, Peace and Godliness,* ch. 5.
8. See E. de Vries, *Man in Rapid Social Change;* Paul Abrecht, *The Churches in Rapid Social Change; Towards a Theology of Development,* SODEPAX, for bibliographies.
9. See *The Family in the Caribbean,* ed. Stanford N. Gerber, Institute Caribbean Studies, University of Puerto Rico 1968.
10. A Mentor Book published by the New American Library by arrangement with UNESCO, 1955.
11. See article by S. C. Parmar in EPS, 3 July 1970.
12. See *The Observer,* 4 October 1970, article by Dennis Bloodworth, 'We Know You Westerners too Well'.
13. See *Risk,* Vol. 6, No. 2, 1970, 'Good Will or Evil Goods', p. 26 (WCC publication).
14. It underlies A. van Leeuwen, *Christianity in World History.*
15. See B. N. Y. Vaughan, *Structures for Renewal,* pp. 36 ff.

Not by Bread Alone - Economic Fallacies

how to make ord.

Two things have become abundantly clear in the developing countries during the past ten years. One of them is that you cannot satisfy the real needs of people only by providing them with more of the physical necessities of life. Economic growth is not the total answer to underdevelopment. The other is that the process itself, by which development goals are achieved, has a great deal to do with the failure to provide that human satisfaction. The point of the first temptation recorded in the gospel is not only that bread alone does not satisfy man's needs. It also is meant to say that the process by which bread is made and supplied has to be respected. The miraculous provision of bread, which was the temptation, by-passes the whole process of producing man's basic requirements, and, in doing so, does violence to him, by ignoring vital elements in the total context of his life. It is with this second fact that we shall deal in this chapter. We shall discuss the lesson which is being learned by those who assumed that economic development would by itself solve the problems of the poorer countries.

The development programmes of the 1950s and 60s started from a primary concern about the condition of people in these countries. Hunger, disease, illiteracy and a number of other human ills, led those in more fortunate circumstances to a new concern about providing the basic amenities of life for the suffering multitudes in other parts of the world. This resulted in an unprecedented emphasis on economic development in these areas and the major effort was directed to this end. We shall briefly look at how it began and what has resulted.

The resolution of the General Assembly of the United Nations 1710 (XVI) which set off its first Development Decade was framed in terms of this concern and purpose. It set as its objective to

accelerate progress towards self-sustaining growth of the economy of the individual nations and their social advancement so as to attain in each under-developed country a substantial increase in the rate of growth, with each country setting its own target, taking as the objective a minimum rate of growth of aggregate national income of 5% at the end of the Decade.

This decision was in turn based on the research and experience accumulated over the previous ten years or so. Looking forward from that experience the United Nations Committee on Programme Appraisals was able to say:

> Great headway has been made in fact-finding and the establishment of internationally comparable statistics and other data. More than a start has been made in ascertaining needs and defining problems which call for action, private and public, national and international. Objectives have been formulated and standards set. Above all through technical assistance a worldwide transfer and interchange of knowledge and technology has been organized, which lies at the very basis of economic and social development. As a result of all this, international organizations have become a potent factor in stimulating action by national governments and assisting them in their efforts to improve economic conditions and raise levels of living.[1]

As the 1960s went by the fallacies of these theories began to appear in the economic experience of the developing countries. The rate of growth proved unsatisfactory, being generally erratic and uneven. Even where the growth rate was more satisfactory, it did not bridge the gap between the poorer and the richer nations. In fact, the gap became wider. Nor again did the rate of growth always show an equivalent *per capita* increase in income. Population growth frequently outstripped that of the economy. Moreover, the economic growth itself had been stimulated by artificial external measures through loans and other means which increased the dependence of these countries on donor nations and deprived them of the capacity to direct and determine their own future. Inside the Third World the shape of their development, the incentives required for development in the form of profits and the connection of privileged groups with the sources of technology created a gap between rich and poor in these countries themselves.

These faults in the economic development process have been the subject of continuous study not only by the United Nations' agencies but also by the churches. The United Nations Conference on Trade and Development held in New Delhi attempted to secure an agreement from the developed nations to a measure of indicative world economic planning, whereby a rational system taking account of the resources and potential of the poorer countries would begin to equalize the wealth of the world as between nations.

Lately, the Pearson Report[2] was issued together with that of the Food and Agricultural Organization[3] as well as the Tinbergen Report.[4] These all called for a better sharing of world resources and a change in economic, political and social structures. In particular the Pearson Report called for an acceleration in the flow of aid from the developed countries to reach a target of at least 1% of their Gross National Product by 1972, of which 75% should be in the form of government grants. The Report called for a liberalizing of the terms of trade giving the developing countries access for their manufactures to the markets of the richer nations, and the stabilizing of prices of those primary commodities which are particularly vulnerable on the world market. Aid should be untied and debts rescheduled.

The recommendations of the various United Nations Organization reports have in the past been generally supported by reports emanating from ecumenical conferences that have followed. The report of the World Conference on Church and Society in 1966[5] followed on that of the United Nations Conference on Trade and Development in 1964[6] and among other things attempted to rally the churches behind the general policy of UNCTAD and UNO. This was succeeded two years later by the Conference on World Co-operation for Development[7] arranged by the World Council of Churches and the Vatican Commission on Justice and Peace where the combined support of the Roman Catholic Church and the World Council of Churches was given to the efforts of the United Nations. It was after that conference that the Joint Committee of the Roman Catholic Church and the World Council of Churches on Society, Development and Peace – SODEPAX – came into being and a new powerful instrument was forged for the churches' involvement in the policy and work of development.

SODEPAX is relatively new on the scene but already it is beginning to speak with an independent voice to the secular organizations which have been involved in development policy and plans. For instance and as a sign of how the church is now taking an independent line, the Montreal conference arranged by SODEPAX in May 1969[8] goes further than simply to support the need for an increase in the volume and quality of aid. It also speaks about the deeper implications of aid, about the human associations in which community involvement and participation take place, and the structures which affirm and deny them and how the Christian must view these. The churches have begun to feel critical of the usual assumptions about economic development being the end of all things.

After Montreal came the annual meeting of SODEPAX at Nemi in Italy in June 1970[9] where one of the work groups reported on 'The Structures of World Justice and Development'. This was followed later by a SODEPAX report on those reports produced by the Pearson Commission, by the FAO, and by Tinbergen, to which we have already referred. What is significant about this report on the reports, entitled *Partnership or Privilege?*[10] is that it states that it can neither accept the analysis of these reports entirely nor all their recommendations. The rate of change adopted in these reports, it says, is too slow, and allows 'enclaves of luxury' to remain. Then it brings out the important truth that economic growth must subserve justice and not be an end in itself.

These reports and others tend to show that the church is no longer content to follow behind the analyses, policies and programmes of secular organizations. It is beginning to realize that there are insights and standards which belong to its own Christian understanding of man and are enshrined in its Bible and teaching by means of which it is able to take an independent look at the development process. It is possible that the ecumenical dimensions which its new organizations have acquired have helped the church to free itself more easily than others from standards and values which belong to western culture from which the development process is guided and dominated.

However, it is only gradually succeeding in doing this since the base of the organized Christian church is still in the West. By a strange irony, which we shall notice later, it is through the connection which Christians have had in recent years with other faiths of the East and with non-Christian ideologies that we have been able to reflect upon the values and standards of our own western Christian culture. This is happening as a result of dialogue between Christians and others which is taking place at an increasing rate in recent years. This dialogue has driven Christians to take another look at the real meaning of their faith and to compare the standards and ideals implicit in it with those of the actual culture and community which Christians share. This has led to considerable social and economic self-criticism on their part. Looking at ourselves in the mirror of the 'law of perfect liberty', that is, against the Christian standards which we profess, we have begun to discover that these by no means measure up to the ideal of humanity to which we have been committed by our faith.

This has led to deep questioning about the standards and values which have been assumed in the development programmes, most of them inspired and initiated from the Christian West. Among others it has caused the basic question to be asked as to what are the cultural values and social standards implicit in development programmes. It is when this question is asked that Christians engaged in the development debate begin to discover that western ideas determine the economic policies promoted over the past twenty years, as they did during the colonial period.

Values and standards which we have assumed can be listed briefly. They form an interrelated complex in which one is derived from and gives support to the other, so that to disentangle them in any social context or culture creates cultural and social complications. This is why the whole complex of values is generally implicit in development programmes. But when they meet another set of values in another culture the impact is sociologically and culturally more disastrous than otherwise. The list of western values would start with individualism, in the sense of emphasis on the individual as the basic unit around which society is organized, rather than on community as the unit in which the individual is included. This leads to private wealth and property as the incentive to effort, class distinction in a separable hierarchy as a symbol of financial success, with the middle class as the means of social stability, and with competition as a method of deciding power, wealth and status.

This list of standards and values, which form the assumptions of our culture, of course, requires a more careful articulation by social scientists and is by no means exhaustive. In broad outline, however, these are some of the criteria which determine our values and control our responses. These criteria and values have entered into development programmes initiated from the West in the Third World and it is necessary to be aware of this important fact in any analysis which Christians make of the programmes themselves and to assess to what extent they are responsible for the disillusion which has followed economic development in much of the Third World. We detect behind that process of turning stones into bread which fails to satisfy human need a set of values and criteria which have been uncritically assumed to be valid.

Over against these criteria there are other values many of which have been retained in one form or another in non-western societies and all of which are implicit in the biblical and Christian understanding of human life. These values are community, making possible human and personal integrity (as distinct from individualism), participation, freedom, spiritual welfare. If these values are denied in the process of turning natural resources into bread, then the distinctively human is not given the sustenance it needs to live. We shall now examine some of the fallacies produced by the assumption of western values in non-western development.

The first fallacy is that economic growth is a primary end of development. Anyone who has lived in a developing country in the last ten years knows the emphasis which is placed by politicians on the economic growth of the country. It is regarded as the measure of success. It has become politically essential, therefore, to show an annual increase in productivity, irrespective of all else.

This criterion has recently come under considerable criticism, not only in Christian circles, but also in those countries where economic growth has not been followed by an increase in economic independence. Economic growth may be accelerated by different kinds of stimuli, but if this is at the expense of basic human values of dignity, freedom and equality, there is no guarantee that it will be maintained.

Dr Charles Elliott who until he became Associate Secretary of SODEPAX worked as an economist at the University of Lusaka in Zambia, has made a study[11] of the relationship of development to economic growth on the one hand and to economic independence on the other. The question which he sets out to answer is whether healthy economic development in the emerging nations can be produced without economic independence, that is, as long as they depend on others for assistance. It is a live question because several states have chosen to seek economic independence rather than any kind of economic growth which requires continued dependence.[12] Instances of this choice cited by Elliott are Chile under Eduardo Frei, who refused United States aid in 1967; Peru has followed a similar policy; Tanzania, under Nyerere,[13] since 1963 has not accepted bilateral aid and foreign capital but has consistently refused any assistance which has political strings attached. Others who have attempted the same policy have been Sekou Touré of Guinea, Kaunda of Zambia, Mobutu of the Congo and Nkrumah of Ghana. Elliott says their attempts have been part of their struggle against any arrangement which seeks to dominate newly independent countries through economic controls.

Elliott goes on to say that there are two distinct relationships which a developing society or entity in its attempt to accelerate economic growth normally has with an external economic power. The relationship may be either that of being dominated by the foreign power or that of being dependent upon it. Where growth is sought without economic independence and where, in consequence, relationships are non-reciprocal between the developing country or sector and the external power which possesses the means of development in the form of skill, finance and markets, growth takes place at the expense of domination or dependence.

He then goes on to describe domination and dependence and their effects in detail. Domination, he says, is usually exercised through large corporations and it is normally expressed through various economic arrangements which they impose on the societies which accept them in the hope of accelerating growth and development.

The arrangements imposed in this way are listed by Elliott as:

> the use of unsuitable forms of economic arrangements, such as
> capital intensive means of production in labour intensive areas.
> For the management and operation of this kind of technology
> there is little local skill and this increases the power of the
> external body to dominate;
> the tendency to increase wages above the national interest. The
> rising wages generally can only be satisfied by increasing capital
> intensive operations which in turn reduce the number of wage-
> earners;
> limiting the processing of raw materials in the developing
> countries. By exporting mining and other raw products the
> opportunity is thrown away of advancing the development of
> the country where these are produced. By putting in the pro-
> cessing plants not only would more labour be employed, but
> more foreign credit would be earned;
> the inflation of the wages of the expatriate employee. This makes
> it difficult to transfer to native employees because of the effect
> on the local economy, and domination is thus continued by
> the external interests;
> internal economic distortion through the introduction of foreign
> machinery which cannot be maintained but which foreign
> salesmen succeed in selling and consultants say are necessary.[14]

Elliott's analysis of the effects of domination accepted by some
developing countries in order to produce economic growth leads him
to conclude that when growth is adopted as a primary objective
without reference to other development needs, the process set in
motion defeats the human ends which growth is designed to satisfy.
The way the bread is made hurts the people it is intended to feed.

Similarly, Elliott's analysis of the effects of dependence as distinct
from domination leads to the same conclusion. A dependent relation
accepted in the interests of economic growth is one where a country
or an entity is dependent on another for the flow of goods, services
or money to it as distinct from domination where a country's own
resources are deployed or controlled by an outside power. Capital,
export earnings, skills and entrepreneurship are the items for which
developing countries are normally dependent on developed countries
and international corporations.

The effects of this dependent relationship are listed by Elliott as:

> limitation of tax revenue and inability to determine terms of
> external investment capital. Here he mentions the humiliating
> experience of dependent countries who have to resort to the

auction of their concessions to the highest bidder in order to
induce the flow of foreign capital;

the policy of banks operating in favour of the richer countries.
Credit policies are then attuned to the needs of the developed
country in which the bank operates;[15]

political and other influences operating in overseas aid deprive
the developing country of control of its destiny;

lowering of prices of primary commodities produced in developing countries as a result of glut, whereas developed countries
are insulated against price fluctuations by stock-piling and the
provision of substitutes through advanced agricultural and
chemical technology. A cruel instance of this is the production
of sugar from beet in European countries which is in some
instances subsidized and protected. The effect is to undersell
the cane sugar of the developing countries by dumping surplus
beet sugar on the world market and so putting sugar workers
out of operation in the Caribbean and other countries. The
manipulation of the market at the metropolitan end increases
the dependence of the country at the production end;

the flow of technical skills. Owing to lack of an education base,
especially in Africa, there is a dearth of technicians to supply
industrial needs in most developing countries. This varies from
place to place, but Zambia is quoted as a particularly unfortunate instance where the exclusive supply of education to
Europeans during the colonial period has increased the dependence of Zambia on foreign technicians in proportion to
its development programmes;

the lack of entrepreneurs whose supply is problematic because
this art is one which is neither conveyed nor encouraged by
normal education processes, but is inclined to be more instinctive and inherited. It is, therefore, usually imported, which
means that developing countries are dependent on outside
sources for the entrepreneur class. Elliott makes some other
interesting reflections on this. He says that foreign entrepreneurs attracted by profits will not undertake the process of
structural transformation required by new social needs. They
will, therefore, contribute to growth but not to the healthy
development process. And yet they are necessary. Further,
while entrepreneurs help import substitutes they do not assist
the next difficult state of development which involves risk,
namely, the establishment of intermediate and basic industries,
such as plants for iron and steel, machine tools, heavy engin-
eering and heavy chemicals.

Some of Elliott's observations are open to question and obscure some of the basic issues. However, his final conclusions are important. Elliott says that in the case of a dependent relationship, the reduction in the flow of resources from outside usually leads to a reduction in the rate of growth and development except where the removal of domination leads to a more rational allocation of resources, which is rare. On the other hand, in the case of domination the removal of external controls and the assertion of economic independence in fact increases the possibility of growth since it makes possible a more rational distribution of resources. In so far as economic domination distorts the allocation of growth and development-creative scarce resources, it follows that both growth and development are accelerated by measures which reduce domination of the developing countries by the developed. This happens, however, only when the removal of external domination is followed by the removal of domination by internal interests which are exercised inside the developing country itself. This is another side of the story.

Elliott's emphasis on the conditions which make rational and integrated development possible is illustrated by William Demas, the General Secretary of the Caribbean Free Trade Association.[16] He says that the weakness of the economy of the Caribbean is due to the lack of integration between sectors of the economy as a result of the restriction of development to a few selected industries for which foreign capital had to be attracted in the interests of growth.

> The penetration of the large international corporations and growth in the mining, tourism and manufacturing sectors indeed led to fairly high rates of economic growth. But an independent self-sustaining process of economic development was not achieved. We must understand the difference between growth and development. The important point to be grasped is that neither growth nor development can be defined in 'value-free' technical terms ... development means not only economic growth but economic growth generated from within a country as well as growth which results in economic diversification in the sense of the creation of more interdependence or 'linkages' between the different industries and activities within a country – a satisfactory level of employment, a fairly equal distribution of income and the greatest possible participation by the people of the country in the economy.

The second fallacy is that development can be measured satisfactorily in terms of *per capita* growth. There are two measurements used by economists to assess rates of development. They are, first, the gross national growth which is assessed by calculating the annual increment in the total earnings of the country or sector. We have looked at some of the fallacies which may be concealed in a development directed purely at economic growth. The second is *per capita* growth. This measures development not simply in terms of the gross increase of the wealth of the country but in terms of the increased amount available to each member of the population. It is known that whereas the gross national product may be increased in a particular country, the increase in population in that country may outstrip the productivity growth, so that the rate of the *per capita* increase may be minus or at least smaller than the percentage national economic growth. *Per capita* growth has, therefore, come to be regarded as a more reliable measure of development, and has led to an awareness in development programmes of the need to control population increase.

What we are concerned with now is to show that *per capita* increase does not in itself provide a reliable criterion of development from the human point of view. It is in fact a variation of the gross growth criterion and being purely quantitative in its valuation it is defective. That development should reflect an increase in wealth in such a way that more is available for each person is of very great importance particularly where there is poverty. For the relief of poverty is a primary process of development since without the provision of the basic necessities of life there is human suffering. The question, however, is whether estimates of growth based on the average per person in the community are reflected in the actual distribution of that wealth. If the gross national increase is not accompanied by an actual increase in the *per capita* consumption of goods in such a way that the poor do have more to eat, better houses to live in, better clothes to wear, and so on, then the *per capita* criterion is misleading.

> The well-being of the people is, of course, a function, not only of the total product or income of the economy, but also of a second dimension: the distribution of this income.[17]

How, then, do actual situations, where *per capita* increases have been registered, stand up to analysis of the actual distribution of new wealth? In developing countries generally the picture is not one of equalization but of an increasing gap between the rich and the poor. While the rich get richer, the poor become poorer. This is usually the result of the introduction of those very techniques which have enabled those countries to register a *per capita* annual increase. These techniques, which are largely in the hands of groups who are orientated towards the western home of technology, have had the effect of putting people out of work and so of increasing the number of unemployed without adequate, and generally without any, on-going compensation. The result is that one sees fabulously wealthy homes being erected in rich residential areas, while the poor unemployed gather in ever-growing shanty towns in the Caribbean and barrios in Latin America.

Studies have recently been made in the Caribbean on the question of income distribution as a result of development. E. Ahiram's comparative method of study, based on an analysis of data available in Jamaica and Trinidad and Tobago, which he compares with the results of analyses made elsewhere, show that the developing countries have the highest inequality of income distribution. He says:

> There can be distinguished three groups of countries: Those with a relatively low coefficient of inequality, ranging between ·33 and ·39. In this group are represented, mainly, the developed countries, like Great Britain, other countries in Western Europe and the United States. The second group with coefficients of ·43 to ·45 includes most of the underdeveloped countries for which this kind of data is available. And then, there is Mexico and Jamaica with the highest recorded inequality of incomes, having a coefficient of over ·50.

That was in 1958. He warns that though the Jamaica distribution is the most unequal which is discoverable, this does not mean that there are not places where it is even more unequal. Jamaica is one of few developing countries which is able to supply the statistics. On the other hand, Trinidad is very close to the distribution in more developed countries. He does not give the reason for this, nor can we pause to suggest why this is so. Unfortunately, also, Ahiram's studies were not designed to show whether the inequality is increasing with development, as is usually thought.

A study of this question has been made by Fuat M. Andic in his *Distribution of Family Incomes in Puerto Rico: A Case Study of the Impact of Economic Development on Income Distribution.*[18] He set out to find out whether the development of the Puerto Rican economy shows that a greater equalization of incomes takes place. He tests the view that inequality is due to economic underdevelopment and that with development the inequality is reduced, as it is in the developed countries. His analysis shows that in Puerto Rico 'the distribution of incomes tends to become more equal as the process of economic development continues'. However, Puerto Rico is a unique economy. Tied as it is to the USA by a special commonwealth relationship, it is not typical of a developing country. A suburb of New York and Miami is not a safe criterion of what happens to the distribution of income as a result of development as it happens in developing countries.

Per capita growth fails to reveal the actual regional or area distribution of income[19] and development. Favoured regions get a disproportionate share of the benefit of development programmes. Some are able to secure the allocation of the more remunerative industries, as well as those that are more healthy and pollution free, while others have to take what they can get or nothing at all. The distribution is frequently based on political considerations and it is often decided not by rational planning but by power pressures, personal influences and prejudices.

Whenever growth is governed by the quantitative principle alone, whether gross or *per capita*, the human factor tends to be violated. Growth alone is not enough. Justice and fair distribution have to become more decisive standards by which development programmes are arranged and assessed. Criticizing the Pearson Report because of the fact that justice is made secondary to economic growth, the SODEPAX report, *Partnership or Privilege?*, says:

> Compassion and justice demand that we start from a perception of what social objectives are minimally acceptable for a life that is consistent with the Christian concept of man created in the image of God. We must, then, work outwards and backwards from that perception to discover what changes must be made in the policies of both the rich countries and the poor to ensure that all men are given access to that quality of life within the foreseeable future.

The third fallacy is that economic development does not require structural changes in order to fulfil its real purpose. It is here that we come up against one of the most difficult issues in the whole development exercise. It is that of identifying what changes need to be made and what follows from that, getting the necessary changes made. Here we shall try to understand what is meant by structural change and in the next chapter we shall deal with the problem of how structural changes are effected.

It will help if we start with the meaning of the word 'structure'. Derived from the Latin *struo*, 'draw up', it refers to the formation of shape which is given to, or adopted by, an entity or a given set of entities. Frequently it refers to the way in which an army is 'drawn up' for battle, which means the relationships which exist between the various military units drawn up for engagement in battle. The way in which these units are drawn up or related to one another determines the course of the battle. In development strategy, the question of structure has acquired a similar importance.

In development studies structure refers to the way in which political and economic entities are arranged. They all have a structure which gives them shape as separate units. But there is also the structural arrangement in which the various economic and political units are related to one another. Just as the army unit has a structure of its own, but also forms part of a larger battle formation.

From this it is not difficult to see that there are two kinds of structural issues in development strategy. There are those structural issues which belong to the separate political and economic entities themselves, like the internal arrangements of the army units. There are also the issues which arise concerning the way in which the economic and political entities are related to one another. However, these issues are interrelated since the relationship between the political and economic entities cannot be changed without changing the internal structures of those entities themselves. Changes in battle formation call for changes in the units themselves which make up the major formation.

What is now being claimed is that it is not possible to have healthy development any more than it is to win a battle unless the whole formation is changed by rearranging the relationships between the economic and political units themselves. As long as the present international structures remain and the existing arrangements between nations continue, healthy development is not possible. This is particularly the case as between developed and developing countries, but as we shall see it also is true between developing nations themselves.

Changes in international relationships, however, mean that changes have to be accepted inside those nations themselves. Economic and political modifications have to be accepted within the nations themselves if they are to have a new kind of relationship to one another. It is the acceptance of these modifications and changes required to make these international relationships possible which causes the main difficulties and raises the problem of how change can be effected. We shall look at this in the next chapter. For it is idle to talk about development unless people are also prepared to accept the changes which it demands.

It is remarkable, therefore, that while at the recent Nemi Consultation[20] the SODEPAX committee looked at some of these structural issues which are raised by development in the relationships between developed and developing countries, yet it did not deal with the changes which would have to be accepted by the nations to make the new relationships possible. For instance, it endorsed the Pearson Report's recommendations concerning the transfer of aid to developing countries, the untying of aid, and the rescheduling of debts. It reiterated the need to improve trade relations by stabilizing prices of primary commodities and liberalizing of trade through access to markets, removal of tariff barriers and other restrictive devices, as well as providing trade preferences and more generous terms to developing countries. It also called for improvement in the investment policies of the rich groups and in arrangements concerning imported technology. This would mean international structural transformation. But all it was able to say about changes within the nations themselves was that its study of international structures had an eye also on 'their implications for justice or injustice as between powerful and underprivileged groups within developing countries'. It did not touch on the internal changes 'because the identification of these national structures for widely varying regions can only be done effectively by those familiar with specific regions or nations'. It is difficult to see how the 'international structural transformation' called for by Nemi can be effected without the internal changes which alone can make this possible.

It is this kind of change of structure which is particularly difficult to make. The resistance from political and economic entities to change their relationships to others is itself difficult enough. Personal interests, traditions, methods of operation and a number of other hidden factors have to be encountered in any attempt at change even at this level. When, however, it is a case of losing their identity or surrendering instruments and, in this way reducing their power to control their own affairs, the resistance is formidably strengthened. Attempts to political federation have failed on this account. The ill-fated federation of the West Indies foundered on the rock of the separate political interests of the various islands, personality problems and the resistances to rearrangements of sovereignty. Private or group vested interests create a strong barrier to the creation of new political and economic structures.

What structural changes, then, are called for to supply the basic human needs for which development is designed, and what are realistic and possible? There are two types of structure which require a measure of modification in the present political and economic arrangements on a world and regional basis and appear to be ripe for consideration and action. The first are those structural changes which increase the self-reliance of developing countries. It is becoming clear that no effective answer can be found for the healthy development of emerging nations as long as they are dependent on the older countries to the extent that they are now. Development demands a measure of real economic independence to enable the emerging nations to plan their own future and to take real responsibility for it. Economic dependence deprives them of this necessary power. To preserve their dignity they have to be in a position to compete on the world market and should not be permanently dependent on concessions. Whatever, therefore, contributes to their self-reliance helps their human dignity in world society.

On the other hand, it is equally obvious that modern economic facts are such that very seldom is it possible to compete realistically in the economic field unless the base which supplies the skills, the finance and the markets is so considerably increased that large-scale economic replanning and integration can take place on a much wider basis than the present small nation states. This is why regional arrangements appear to be essential to the economic progress of the developing countries.[21] This is also why CARIFTA, The Caribbean Free Trade Association, and the Central American Common Market as well as LAFTA, Latin American Free Trade Association, are so important to the future of territories in the Caribbean. As for the developed countries and large finance corporations operating from the richer countries, this imposes upon them the requirement that they adopt policies which will encourage rather than inhibit these regional arrangements. For it is comparatively easy, through the finance and skills owned by them, for the developed countries to exercise pressures and temptations which will destroy these regional arrangements, and so divide and rule. It is easy, for instance, for a corporation in the USA to tie up an economy in Latin America or the Caribbean in such a way as to make it an ineffective member of CARIFTA or LAFTA and in this way to reduce the self-reliance which these countries can get only through their regional association.

The second type of structural change which is needed is that which contributes to the rational expression of world interdependence. The world is already interdependent because of its economic and technical arrangements. However, the form in which this interdependence is expressed in present world structures is defective and does not contribute towards the sense of world community which is a necessary corollary of world interdependence. The United Nations Organization offers a forum on which many of the problems of the developing countries can be discussed and a place where pressures can be exercised. It may very well be the nucleus of the formation of a world community. However, before that becomes a reality considerable structural transformation will have to take place, and this is likely to take time to evolve. We have already seen how this evolution may happen in the areas of aid and trade.

There is another area which has recently been receiving attention from the churches. It is the area of monetary reform. In February 1970, a colloquium was sponsored by SODEPAX in Geneva on 'The Interests of the Developing Countries and International Monetary Reform'.[22] What follows is an attempt to summarize the conclusions and information supplied in the report of that colloquium, having in mind the expression of the evolution of world interdependence in terms of monetary relationships. This evolution began with the formation of the International Monetary Fund after World War II in 1944 at Bretton Woods.

It was created to provide a medium to assist liquidity and equilibrium for the governments which joined the Fund then or subsequently. Members have been able to draw in foreign currency 200% of the quota paid by them into the fund to meet balance of payments difficulties. Arrangements have also been made for Special Drawing Rights since 1970 to meet balance of payment problems. Though these SDR's benefit the industrial countries, they also indirectly help the developing countries since in this way the rich countries are able to balance their payments and give aid to the poorer countries. The IMF is also able to exercise influence on the values of currency which is particularly important for exchange in trading arrangements and on equating the value of currencies with the actual reserves held. It provides a financial and monetary forum where these problems can be settled by a complicated voting process which has been devised to express the interests of the members according to their quota payment.

Leading up to the Special Drawing Rights arrangement implemented in 1970, there were other monetary reforms which helped to ease the position of the developing countries. These are listed by J. B. Zulu, economic adviser to the President of Zambia, as:

First, the stand-by arrangements established in 1952 by IMF. This is a facility for assisting on a temporary basis members of the Fund who are facing balance of payments difficulties. Established for the benefit of both developed and developing countries, the latter have benefited more in proportion to their volume of business than the developed countries from this arrangement.

Secondly, there was the compensatory finance facility established in 1962 to assist primary producers facing persistent fluctuations in their export incomes. They may draw from the Fund whenever their earnings fall below a medium term trend. By 1969, three billion dollars had been drawn on the Fund under this scheme. This indicates both the vulnerability of the developing countries, which are the main primary producers, and the benefit which this arrangement has brought them.

Thirdly, there has been the help offered by IMF in the international stabilization of primary prices. In 1969 a new facility was established for financing the contribution to approved international buffer stocks. The intention of this is to mitigate the price fluctuations which hit primary producers. The arrangement allows a member to draw 50% of its quota in any twelve months, but the combined drawings for price stabilization and compensatory financing may not exceed 75% and repurchase has to be undertaken from three to five years.

Fourthly, outside the IMF there have been the Federal Reserve 'swop' arrangements set up to re-route financing in respect of seasonal flows. By discouraging speculative attacks on beleaguered currencies, this has helped to stabilize currencies, thus removing financial limitations on developing programmes. There is the Bank of International Settlements whose direct and indirect influence in mitigating and promoting reform in and outside the IMF is well-known. There are the swops among European Central Banks whose incidence has increased in recent years and which have added flexibility and adaptability to the system by providing readily available short-term international credit to those Central Banks which are in need.

Finally, in 1968, the Bâle Agreement gave support to the pound sterling and showed what possibilities there are in international monetary co-operation.[23]

The limitations of the IMF are that the voting rights being geared to quota payment gives insufficient representation to the under-developed countries. This means that the full meaning of world economic interdependence is insufficiently expressed. The suggestion put forward by Professor Triffin,[24] that monetary issues should be regionalized and the IMF decentralized, has been criticized by J. Marquez,[25] because there are not many common financial decisions between industrialized countries, which can be considered of purely regional interest, and the policies of these developed countries are not likely to be influenced by representations from these regional groupings. Nevertheless, the IMF offers a way forward by gradual evolution towards effective monetary control, which will take care of the poorer nations of the world, which are most vulnerable to currency decisions made by the wealthy nations.

NOTES

1. See *Five-Year Perspective 1960–1964*, quoted in *The United Nations Development Decade*, p. 3.
2. *Partners in Development*, UN 1969.
3. *Indicative World Plan for Agricultural Development*, UN 1970.
4. *Towards Accelerated Development*, UN 1970.
5. WCC 1966.
6. UN 1964.
7. *World Development: Challenge to the Churches*, SODEPAX 1968.
8. *The Challenge of Development*, SODEPAX 1969.
9. See Committee on Society, Development and Peace, *The Plenary Meeting*, June 21–27 1970 (The Nemi Report), SODEPAX 1970.
10. SODEPAX 1970.

11. See *Study Encounter*, Vol. V, No. 2, 1969, pp. 54ff.

12. See Tom Mboya, *Freedom and After*.

13. See *African Socialism*, ed. W. Freedland and C. G. Rosberg, Stanford UP and OUP 1964, p. 51.

14. For an amusing account of this process, see I. M. D. Little, *Aid to Africa*, pp. 21, 22, *et passim*.

15. Little, p. 66.

16. In a paper prepared for the SODEPAX Consultation held in Trinidad in November 1971, 'Political Economy of English-speaking Caribbean'.

17. See the essay by E. Ahiram, 'Income Distribution in Jamaica and Trinidad-Tobago' in *The Caribbean in Transition*, ed. F. M. Audic and T. G. Matthews, p. 1.

18. See 'Caribbean Monograph Series', Institute of Caribbean Studies, University of Puerto Rico 1964.

19. Ahiram, art. cit., p. 7, shows that the *per capita* income in urban areas in Jamaica is much higher than in rural areas.

20. See *The Plenary Meeting* (The Nemi Report), pp. 1–5.

21. See *Caribbean Integration*, ed. Sybil Lewis and Thomas Matthews, and Aaron Segal, *The Politics of Caribbean Economic Integration*.

22. See *Money in a Village World*, SODEPAX 1970.

23. See *Money in a Village World*, pp. 74ff.

24. Robert Triffin, *The World Money Maze: National Currencies in International Payment*, Yale UP 1966, quoted in *Money in a Village World*, p. 56.

25. Op cit., p. 57.

3

Change or Decay - The Dynamics of Peace

In the first chapter we said that economic development entailed two kinds of changes. There are those changes which follow inevitably from economic development.[1] There are also those changes which are required to be made to meet the inevitable effects of new economic enterprise in order not only to safeguard social health and other human needs, but also to promote development itself. It is with this second set of changes that we propose to deal in this chapter under the title 'Change or Decay'.

In saying this we are begging the question. There are two views on this subject. There is the view that the effects of economic change should be allowed to take care of themselves. Adam Smith's *laissez-faire* doctrine envisaged a natural law which works through the motive of self-interest and by its own operation produces the adaptations which are required to meet the effects of economic causes. Economic laws must, therefore, not be interfered with; otherwise they will not work effectively.

Laissez-faire doctrine raises both economic and moral issues which it is not our intention to discuss here. It is sufficient to state that from the moral point of view the tendency now is to stress the implications of human responsibility for the shape which the economic order takes. This assumption, it is true, carries with it other implications which raise important issues. These, again, are beyond our scope here. For instance, the type of society which is desirable and the essential nature of man to which such planning should be directed raise very big issues. There are also questions about the possible and the practicable. However, having these issues in mind the assumption which we make is that human responsibility is not compatible with *laissez-faire* as it is commonly understood.

Similarly, economics present us with theories and questions which it would be presumptuous to judge. Economic factors alone, quite apart from the social and political context in which they operate, cover an enormous field where differences of opinion exist between economists. From Adam Smith through Keynes and Marx to Galbraith is a long way. All we can say here is that what Galbraith[2] has written about economic theories does not encourage us to accept the view that we are to bow down before any theory which limits unduly human capacity to change the economic order by the exercise of responsible judgment and will. The ecological problems and the political dangers to peace stress the importance of human responsibility in economic and political decisions.

We seem, therefore, to be committed to the view that man is responsible for effecting such changes as are required to enable him to have a society where he is free, and his dignity, equality and welfare are assured. We are compelled also by experience to face the need to use human initiative to make certain structural changes on a national and international level.

This raises the question of what changes should be made and how they can be effected. The question of what precise changes need to be made is one which has to be left to experts in the various relevant fields. From the theological point of view we can go no further than to say that such structural changes need to be made as will enable people to have the maximum freedom, equality, dignity and means of living, and that these are best guaranteed by structures which express human interdependence, community, sharing and effective participation in the control of their destiny.

What makes it difficult to effect changes which produce these results is the fact that power in the form of wealth, political control, military weapons, knowledge and skill, are vested in particular groups and individuals either within the nations themselves or within the total global situation. The present structures which form and determine human life are shaped along the lines of these power areas. They are designed to serve these interests. They are, therefore, very difficult to change because they contain the vested interests of individuals, groups and nations. Moreover, no one normally voluntarily surrenders a privileged position. He has to be persuaded either by the compulsion of a superior power or by self-interest, to accept changes which redistribute power or wealth which are now within his own control.

An example of the need to change economic structures can be given from Latin America. It is widely known that most Latin American countries are faced with problems of social and economic inequality. Oppression, poverty and under-development are the consequences of the economic structures of many of these countries which are upheld by tradition and sanctioned by legal constitutions, sometimes with religious supports, as in the case of land which is inalienable because it has been dedicated. During the last twenty years there has been growing dissatisfaction with the traditional pattern and a refusal to accept poverty as an inevitable lot in life. The so-called revolution of rising expectations has been stirred by the new communication media which have shown the people the possibilities of a better life. But before poverty can be defeated, the economic structures have to be changed. The land has to be redistributed and cultivated. Other structures have to be changed also. This is what development means in Latin America.

Structural change has, therefore, become a prominent concern of the churches of Latin America. There are two movements which illustrate two different approaches in Latin America to getting change effected. The first is that of the Evangelical churches, under the title ISAL, which have organized themselves to discuss and present a common front on development issues. Several meetings have been held during the last ten years, which have led these churches to the conclusion that the lot of the people can only be improved if political structures are changed. ISAL claims that the fault lies in the political organization where the power is centred. It has, therefore, opted for political action. ISAL says of itself[3]:

> In Piriapolis, ISAL defined itself as an 'intermediate group' whose task is to prepare vanguard groups in the Latin American society for political action. That is, in ISAL's history, the development of our countries has been seen as something which can only come about through revolution, a demand which the Christian cannot avoid, because it is only through the liquidation of the system of oppression that man can be really human, free from all alienating limitations. From its early reformist stage, ISAL passed rapidly and decidedly to take a revolutionary option.

The other approach is that of the Latin American Catholic Episcopal College, CELAM, which has been active since 1955. It is not always clear how far their diagnosis of the political causes of injustice in Latin America commits CELAM to the revolutionary option. At Medellin in 1968, the majority appeared in favour of this means of liberation as a key to justice, and the second chapter of their document says:

> They are responsible, too, for injustice – all those who do not act to bring justice about to the extent that they have the means to do so, and remain quiet out of the fear of the sacrifices and personal risks which are implicit in every audacious and truly efficacious action.[4]

But on the whole, the bishops hesitate about the uses of violent revolution. While they do not cut it out completely, their option is mainly that of their meeting at Mar del Plata in 1966, that is, they defend a 'reform of social structures, but one which would be gradual and assimilable by all, and would be brought about together unanimously'.[5]

The Roman Catholic bishops' approach is, therefore, one which effects change more by appeal to the mass of the people, who, of course, are Roman Catholic in their allegiance, than by direct political action. They hope for a change from within, by appeal to enlightened self-interest.

We, therefore, make an urgent call to private businessmen and political authorities to radically modify their attitudes and methods with respect to the finality, organization and functioning of business. It is on them that social and economic change in Latin America fundamentally depends.[6]

We cannot affirm that this approach of CELAM is entirely unrealistic. Eduardo Frei, in 1967, was motivated by his Catholic allegiance and realism about the situation in Chile, and was able by democratic processes to effect changes there, not only in the international relations of that country, but internally also. It has yet to be discovered, however, whether this democratic process which put in the Marxist President Allende to succeed Frei will continue to be followed in Chile.

We do know, however, that this approach has come under considerable criticism in Latin America, not only from the more revolutionary elements, but also from those who have a deep acquaintance with the political and economic structures of those countries. The rejection of the gradual approach through appeal and moral persuasion has been part of the criticism which has been made of the Pope's own approach which is described as *desarrollismo*.

Desarrollismo can be translated 'developmentism'. It is a pejorative word to distinguish it from *desarrollo*, 'development'. It emphasizes the theoretic, unrealistic approach to change which, for that reason, does not produce real development. This, it is claimed, requires stronger action and more immediate and effective involvement in changing the structures of Latin American society. *Desarrollismo* has, therefore, become a bad word in these circles.

This is how the debate is conducted in Latin America about the alternatives frequently described in other parts of the world as revolution, reform and radicalism. These are the alternatives envisaged elsewhere. This might be a suitable point at which to discuss them.

Strictly speaking radicalism is not a method of effecting change. It is, rather, an attitude towards change. It means going to the roots. So that a radical in development would desire change to take place at the roots or at the very base of society, whether political, economic or social.

> Radicalism is not a clearly defined band in the political spectrum so much as an attitude or temper of mind ... Radicalism represents the built-in challenge to any establishment, any institutionalism, any orthodoxy ... The radical's response is to go to the roots – hence his name. It is to ask what the Sabbath is for, what human values it exists to frame, and then to try to see, at whatever cost to the institution of the orthodoxy, that it does so.[7]

While radicalism is, therefore, an attitude which also provides motivation towards change, it does not prescribe the means by which change will be effected.

Revolution, on the other hand, is concerned with the means by which change is promoted. The word revolution means 'to turn round' or 'change position', and now is commonly associated with change in the control of power. It means action taken to move the centre of power from one group or person to another. It also means the introduction of new centres of power which affect the total organization of society. This is the sense in which we speak of the technological revolution, where new means of production affect the economy and the whole social scene; or again, the student revolution, which introduces students as a new power centre.

Since political control normally decides the use of power in any society, revolution is generally associated with political action of some kind, normally with the transference of political power so that it is not exercised by or confined to the same people. Latin America is noted for its revolutions in this sense of the term, but it is not particularly noted for effecting social revolution as a result of the change of political power.

It is for this reason that political revolution is no longer regarded in Latin America as sufficient to provide what is required to bring about the changes called for by economic development. An economic revolution is also being demanded. This means a change in the control over economic resources and processes, particularly the system of land tenure.

Over against revolution stand the advocates of 'reform' as a means of changing the structures of human life. Reform, basically, means giving a new shape to something. Again, it has no moral connotation, but refers simply to changing the formation or structure which is possessed by an organization or institution. This can be appreciated by writing the word with a hyphen, re-formation. Whereas the revolutionary wishes to change the total structure of society, the reformer accepts certain structures as basic and makes his changes within or in relation to these. In this way, he also proposes to do it peacefully and painlessly.

The criticism levelled against the reformer, or 'reformist', to use the pejorative form, particularly in Latin America, is that his reforms do not touch the real cause of the evils of society. It is the basic structure, both economic and political, that is regarded as in need of change in those countries, and any reform within it is regarded by many as merely a palliative and a means of continuing the suffering of the poor, disfranchized, illiterate masses. In recent years the church itself has been challenged to make its own position clear in relation to this particular debate. Does it support the complete revolution of Latin American society and so the means by which this can be done? Or does it prescribe that the changes which must take place need not necessarily change the basic political and economic structures themselves? ISAL comes out clearly in favour of the former; CELAM, hesitatingly, opts for the latter.

The Christian church is, therefore, faced with a moral issue on which a decision has to be made to assist Christians in their political action. It is difficult because the principles are clear but the action demanded is not obvious. The fundamental principle with which Christian social ethics begin is love. This means that all Christian action must be governed by the need to respect the personality, dignity and well-being of all other people. Within the context of Christian moral thought, this basic principle is unquestioned. Nor do enlightened Christians question the corollary of this, that love must be translated into justice, which means that rights are not only conceded to people but that people also have an effective claim on them, legally, economically and politically. But what does this mean in practice?

There is also a second prescription of Christian social ethics derived from biblical thought and based on experience. It is that human dignity, welfare and freedom can only be attained through what the Bible calls 'peace' or *shalom*. The context in which love is effective is that of peace. In fact, the Christian gospel implies this by announcing peace as the gift of God to men, and so providing the context within which love can be expressed. For these reasons peace has always been a prescriptive principle in Christian ethics. But what again does this mean in the context of changing economic structures?

It is for this reason that Christian social ethics have been widely questioned. In the face of contemporary social, economic and political realities, a peaceful attitude condones injustice. And Christians are under criticism because their emphasis on the need for peace has led them to accept unjust situations and to refuse to change these because they are committed to peace.

This criticism is further encouraged by the Christian social tradition which has placed a high value on order. Since the Constantinian Settlement when the church became the moral guardian of the political and social establishment, one of its primary concerns has been the preservation of order. This concern has been accepted not simply as a political expedient to preserve the *status quo* and privileged position of the church in western society, but as a reasoned conclusion from the experience that man is more secure in an ordered society than in one whose stability is threatened even by forces which are not inimical to him. So it is that law and order find an instinctive response in Christian circles.

In recent years, however, the obvious injustices of the international order, as well as the inequalities and distortions within the national structures, have led many Christians to ask whether they are bound to the needs of order and peace, or whether they must obey the demands of justice. For this reason the whole concept of peace has come under scrutiny, and as peace or reconciliation is essential to the ministry of the church in the world, this question has become one of the most important issues of the contemporary debate about revolution and change. In much of what follows I am indebted to a recent publication of the World Council of Churches on this subject, entitled *Conflict, Violence and Peace,*[8] which is a report of a consultation on 'Alternatives to Conflict in the Quest for Peace', held at the Ecumenical Institute in Bossey, Switzerland, in the summer of 1969.

The concept of peace is found in various cultures of the world, and the content of the concept or its orientation tends to vary from culture to culture. In eastern culture the emphasis is on the state of mind. The Indian santi, Chinese ping ho and Japanese heiwa, stress the idea of tranquillity of mind, each, however, in relation to its own cultural assumptions. In Graeco-Roman culture the emphasis is on the maintenance of good order conveyed by the words *eirene* and *pax*. Hebrew and biblical culture, however, stresses the importance of justice and the quality of relationships.[9] All of these ideas are essential ingredients of peace and due regard should be paid to each of these basic human needs, such as the realization of justice, maintenance of good order and tranquillity of mind, in any application of the concept of peace to the development of human society. It is important to say this because the rediscovery of the authentic Judeo-Christian idea of peace which, in its original culture, was itself the result of a balance of complementary stresses, could be easily misinterpreted and misapplied. With that caution let us see what has been rediscovered about the Judeo-Christian idea of peace.

Hebrew thought uses dynamic concepts, and for this reason, peace is not conceived as a state of mind or as an established order. It refers to a particular quality of relationship. It is established between God and man by a covenant which creates the right relationship between them, and it is found in human society when proper relationship exists between its members or between groups. Essential to this relationship is righteousness or justice. So that without justice there is no peace. There is no *shalom*, or well-being, without justice.

Peace, therefore, requires a continuous struggle for justice, and in this respect it contradicts itself, but in doing so it comes into being. Peace, therefore, cannot be understood in Christian thought as involving absence of conflict or tension. In fact, the presence of conflict may be necessary to peace because in the conflict the concealed tensions in human society are exposed and so the parties in tension are able to confront one another with their just claims.

Peace is not merely the absence of war and collective acts of violence; rather, the concept of peace also implies the concept of justice, freedom and development. For if peace was merely defined as the absence of war and collective acts of violence, it will be quite compatible with unjust social conditions, political dictatorship and economic exploitation. Action promoting peace would thus not aim at eliminating the causes leading to conflict; it will merely try to eliminate their after-effects. Thus, a concept of peace which looks deeper than the symptoms must take due account of justice, freedom and development.[10]

Because peace consists in right relationships within the nation and with other nations, and because these relationships must make for justice, economically and socially, we have to accept tension and conflict as a necessary means of establishing these relationships. Peace is broken not by conflict, but only when conflict expresses itself in war and the mutual determination to exterminate one another. This is because destruction of the other party takes the place of a relationship with him wherein he makes a claim on the one with whom he is in conflict. Creative conflict is not a state of war. It is a state of opposition between two parties where their contradictory interests are exposed to one another. It does not exclude the possibility of resolving those differences. When conflict is not allowed, injustice cannot be corrected.

This means that in preaching the gospel of peace the church must not exclude the possibility of creative conflict but accept its possibility and admit it as a possible means of establishing right relationships. The conditions under which these relationships can be established, through the expression of conflicting interests by differ-

ent parties, are democratic processes of decision, and effective
processes of communication between the different parties involved.
It means that other means of establishing peace, such as the use
of superior power, or suppression of the expression of the needs
of the weaker party through persuasion, or depriving them of the
means of putting forward their case through the usual facilities of
communication, would be wrong. Reconciliation, or making peace,
involves opening up lines of communication between conflicting
interests and allowing full expression of the grievances and ambitions of all.

The church can do this; in two ways in particular. The first is by
supplying the means of meeting between the conflicting interests.
The means by which conference, dialogue, research facilities into
the situation, are made possible should, therefore, become priority
claims on the churches' finances and personnel. The second is to
give active support to the idea of confrontation and to withhold
the expression of abhorrence at the fact of any kind of conflict in
any situation. If the church is able to say that confrontation is
right and creative conflict is possible, this will be a tremendous
moral encouragement to the opening up of frank communications.
Conflict, tension and communication express the dynamics of the
peace which is kissed by righteousness.

What, then, is the church's proper attitude towards violence? In
the context of the Christian understanding of peace as a dynamic
achievement of right relationships, through communication, involving the possibility of conflict and tension between parties with
initially opposed interests, any means adopted to resolve the conflict which subdues or destroys or puts undue pressure on the other
party, is a breach of the peace. It eliminates the possibility of right
relationships. War was for centuries regarded as a legitimate method
of resolving disputes and conflicts. But war implies that communications have broken down and that conflict is to be decided by
force rather than by rational means. In involves the attempt to
subjugate or destroy one of the parties in the relationship. It is
a denial of the possibility of reconciliation as a means of establishing proper relationships. War, therefore, in itself is a wrong means
of resolving conflict. There are other uses of war which we do not
propose to discuss here, such as the just war. But the possibility
even of this is now widely questioned in the light of the destructive
potential of nuclear and chemical methods of war.

The problem of alternative methods of establishing justice and
changing structures which impede healthy human development has
to be considered by the Christian in the light of their contribution
to the establishment and maintenance of communications between
conflicting parties. Without communications proper relationships

cannot be established. Conflict and tension imply that communications exist in a potential form. When violence is used, however, it means that communications are breaking down and force takes the place of reason as a method of resolving conflict.

Now it is common in modern discussions, even in Christian circles, to justify violence on the grounds that violence is built into the oppressive structures that now maintain an unjust order. An example of this is the use of the police force by oppressive political regimes, for instance, in South Africa, Brazil and Czechoslovakia. It is being claimed that the use of violence to maintain these oppressive structures, evoking such expressions as 'police brutality', 'police state', 'dictatorship', calls for the counter use of violence to stake the claims of justice. This raises two questions – whether the use of violence is morally right and whether it is expedient. Its ethical quality, of course, very largely depends in particular instances on the second question, because what is not expedient is seldom right.

The use of violence to effect change has, therefore, been a prominent subject in World Council of Churches, and now in SODEPAX, discussions. It is important as well as interesting to note the change of opinion which seems to appear during the 1960s. Before then the question of the use of violence as a national issue was hardly discussed by the church. It was confined to international political issues rather than to intra-national social conflict. This is possibly because until that time the church did not take account of the power structures of modern society, and the possible need of the use of force to change them.

Gradually, however, the idea of power structures within national society was brought forward as a premise in discussion; a gradual evolution of thought starts. In 1961 the World Assembly of the World Council of Churches at New Delhi advised against the use of violence. Instead, it initiated a study programme on the use of non-violent means of producing both moral and structural change in society. Similarly, the Consultation called at Kitwe in 1964 on 'Christian Practice and Desirable Action in Social Change and Race Relations in Southern Africa' expressed its alarm at the use of violence in the interests of racial justice. However, it also noted disagreements about the possible use of violence as a Christian option.

A further step was taken by the World Conference on Church and Society in Geneva in 1966. It recognized violence as a means being used to repress 'the invisible violence perpetrated on people who by their millions have been, or still are, the victims of repression and unjust social systems'. It added that 'it cannot be said that the position of the Christian is absolute non-violence'. But whenever it is used, it must be seen as 'an ultimate recourse which is justified only in extreme situations'.

When the World Council of Churches later took up the theological and moral issues of the Geneva Conference at its Consultation in Zagorsk it produced this frequently repeated formula:

> Christians in the revolutionary situation have to do all in their power to exercise the ministry of reconciliation to enable the revolutionary change to take place non-violently, or, if this is not possible, with the minimum of violence. But we must realize that some Christians find themselves in situations where they must, in all responsibility, participate fully in the revolution with all its inevitable violence.

On the other hand, the Vatican II decree, *Gaudium et Spes*, praised all those who renounced violence in movements for social justice, and the Papal statement in *Populorum Progressio* warned against violence on the grounds that the evil it produced outweighed any good that might come from it.

The Conference called by the World Council of Churches and the Papal Commission, Justice and Peace, in Beirut in 1968, while it did not encourage the use of violence and advised the use of non-violent methods of changing the social structures, said nevertheless:

> But as a last resort men's conscience may lead them in full and clear-sighted responsibility without hate or rancour to engage in violent revolution.

The Assembly of the World Council of Churches at Uppsala in the same year, reflected the more cautious thinking of delegates from the churches. It decided to set aside what was said in the Draft for Sections prepared beforehand for the Assembly which was more open to the use of violence than the eventual agreed report. Uppsala was, of course, fully conscious of the problem of violence as a means of social justice. Its statements on the subject, however, were hesitant and not clear. For example, Section III says 'Law and order may be a form of violence and revolution is morally ambiguous'; Section IV says that both violence and inaction come under judgment; Section VI mentions the 'bloodshed of the *status quo*'. It was quite clear, however, that Uppsala opted for non-violent methods as was shown by the adoption of the Martin Luther King resolution.

The next conference to deal with this subject was that at Notting Hill in May 1969 on Racism. It urged the World Council of Churches to adopt the position 'that all else failing, the Church and Churches, support resistance movements, including revolutions, which are aimed at the elimination of political and economic tyranny which makes racism possible'. It stressed the need for power to be shared with the powerless in the struggle for a better social order.

The SODEPAX Consultation on Peace, held in Baden in April 1970, marks the climax so far of this growing consciousness about the use of violence in the social struggle. It encouraged the churches in Southern Africa 'to resist with all possible means those demands of the social system which conflict with Christian conscience'. The subsequent decision of the World Council of Churches to give financial support to those who have suffered as a result of their resistance to the South African regime has brought the subject of violence on the conference tables of all the churches. Though we have been assured that the World Council of Churches decision was not to support resistance movements themselves but those victims of their own conscience who had been involved in violence and the social aspects of combating racism,[11] there is some doubt left in some minds, and it really centres on Christian support, directly or indirectly, of subversive violence in the cause of justice.

Now that we have looked briefly at the history of the debate on violence in the church, let us at this point take stock of where the problem stands. We have seen that strong pressures are being exercised from within Christian circles, particularly in Latin America, for changing the structures which are causing people to live in poverty, misery and underdevelopment. There is a considerable body of opinion which holds that these structures cannot be changed by an appeal to the voluntary action of those who benefit from the *status quo*. We have also seen that the Christian insistence on peace and love as the necessary context of social organization and personal relationships does not mean that Christians must passively accept the present order. This is because peace is not tranquil passivity but a dynamic relationship whereby people are sustained by goodwill in the conflict which must necessarily arise between the privileged and the underprivileged in the struggle for justice. Peace keeps the lines of communication open and eliminates recrimination and destructive use of force and violence.

All this is very good and most Christians will accept it. The problem really arises at the point where the kind of conflict which is expressive of peace fails to change the *status quo*, when those in power will not yield, and the crowd is calling for violence. This is the real problem. Is violence a viable means of changing the structures of society?

Let us consider, therefore, what those who criticize violence say. These can be divided into four groups. There are those who have a vested interest in the *status quo*. It is normal to discard whatever they say as so tainted with selfishness that it is not worthy of consideration. It is doubtful whether this is a wise way to proceed. Peace means keeping lines of communication open, and dialogue can be a way of producing relationships where change begins be effected. Self-righteous arrogance on the part of those who espouse the cause of justice can defeat the very cause which they uphold. The cause of dynamic peace is not served by the weakness which refuses to confront those on the other side, however wicked they may appear to be. Then there are those who believe that the church should not be involved in economic and political issues on the grounds that this compromises its ministry of reconciliation. The church may indeed not be competent to judge economic and political issues, but when misery and poverty are the result, while it does not encourage the use of violence, it should be clear that the ministry of reconciliation does not require the church to be silent. Reconciliation without justice is not dynamic reconciling peace. It is to condone injustice, and that destroys peace and reconciliation. However, this does not tell us whether violence is a viable instrument. So we turn to the other objectors. They are the pacifists who by conscience are opposed to the use of force, and, lastly, those who consider that the use of violence is counter-productive.

In connection with pacifism and the claim that violence is counter-productive, let us look at the question whether non-violent methods do effect their purpose. Adam Roberts in an article entitled 'Non-violent Resistance as an Approach to Peace',[12] recommends the use of what he calls 'civilian defence'. He describes this as a non-violently operated method of non-co-operation and resistance in which the population as a whole participate to remove oppression and military occupation. He gives instances of the successful use of this method, such as the Wolfgang Kopf military putsch in Berlin in 1920 which had to be abandoned because of civilian resistance; the resistance movement in German occupied territories in Europe during World War II and the withdrawal of French military units from Algiers in 1961 as a result of the same kind of resistance. He quotes Liddell-Hart[13] who describes the purpose of strategy as designed to undermine the enemy by demoralization, over-extending his resources, weakening his economy, creating political problems. The will of the opponent to take reprisals is further weakened by fraternization, propaganda and appeal. Then there was Gandhi's successful non-violent policy which led to independence for India. On the other hand, oppressive regimes have found ways to counter these tactics. For instance, during the Hungarian revolution in 1956, the Russian soldiers who had fallen for these tactics were soon removed and others, ignorant of the Hungarian situation, were sent to quell the revolution. The Czechoslovak incident is another more recent instance of the failure of non-violent resistance.

In the military situations just cited, non-violence has been shown to succeed only in some instances. In others, it does not effect its purpose. The same is true in social situations where non-violent methods are used. Student and workers' demonstrations, black power protests, anti-Vietnam war demonstrations, have had decisive results in some areas of concern within democratic societies, such as the USA. On the other hand, their effect is negative in non-democratic countries and their power to change even the structures of democratic societies has not been demonstrated sufficiently to say that non-violence is a viable means of achieving structural change. Nevertheless, non-violence does have the positive value of reducing the use of violence by the opponent and preventing the hardening of attitudes which would make reconciliation impossible.

David Gill[14] has attempted an assessment of the debate and observed that the difficulties arise out of the desire to establish general guidelines with universal applicability when situations in fact vary so much. He also observes that the separation of violence and non-violence as two exclusive categories tends to conceal the fact that there are various forms and degrees of coercion which are appropriate to different situations. There is also a number of loose terms used, such as 'bloodless violence' and the application of the description 'violence' to any form of injustice. This complicates discussion. Equally, the term 'non-violent' has emotive connotations. Some suspect concealed interest in preserving the *status quo* on the part of those who oppose violence. It can, however, mean not simply refraining from violence but active participation in movements for justice of a non-retaliatory kind with redemptive effects.

Gill suggests instead some criteria by which strategies for action could be more accurately appraised. The first criterion is: What are the likely consequences of a particular course of action? Will it, in fact, effect the desired change? Will it bring retaliation in a form which will cause greater suffering than the situation which the action is designed to remedy? The second criterion is: What are the motives for the action proposed? How is the self-interest of those involved in the action to be controlled in favour of achieving the ends originally sought? The third criterion is the need to effect reconciliation. The action taken should not be such as to make it impossible or difficult to reconcile the parties concerned and to secure their co-operation in the social effort which must go on. The fourth criterion is allegiance to a higher authority than that which is exercised by temporal advantage or society itself. Action designed to effect social change cannot be sustained unless it is the result of obedience to an authority beyond the change itself.

It is significant then, that church statements on the use of violence to effect change are very hesitant. While there may be situations where force can be used with moral justification, recent Christian reflection does not easily entertain the idea. The reason is clear. It is because violence and reconciliation are usually incompatible. Violence is a divisive force in society. Being divisive it does not contribute to human development which is only achieved through community co-operation and the feeling of interdependence of one section of the community on the other. This is the damaging criticism against revolution, as it is generally conceived, in the sense of a change in the centres of power through the exercise of force or violence. It is that violence alienates those whose co-operation is needed to create and sustain a viable society. The purpose of a valid revolution is to improve the economic and social condition of the people. Such an improvement requires in modern days the co-operation of the technocrats, the industrialists, the labour unions, the administration and other sections of society. Any action which alienates these from one another invites failure. This is why a necessary revolution requires reconciliation to make it a success and why violence compromises what it tries to effect.

David Jenkins put it another way. Writing about the 'power of the powerless' in the theological consultation on development at Cartigny[15] in 1969, he referred the question of the use of power to the biblical understanding of poverty and weakness. He says

The basic question is: How seriously do we have to take the Jesus Christ who is portrayed in the gospels as a real embodiment in historical conditions of the presence and power of the Kingdom of God?

On the face of it, the presentation of the New Testament is that when God gets down to work on earth in a personal and definitive manner he exhibits his power in powerlessness. The forsaken and crucified man is believed to be the Christ of God. The New Testament appears to be built on the conviction that Jesus is the way God works.

This appears to suggest that the ultimate power which is capable of bringing in and establishing the Kingdom of God is the love of God, (the God who is love), which love exhibits its power as powerlessness ...

Power as we know it (powerful power and not powerless power) always involves counter-action and counter-effects. Oppression forces either despair or revolt. Revolution produces counter-revolution or else the revolutionaries become counter-revolutionary to hold on to their power.... Wrath creates new waves of resentment.

If we are ever to get to a state of equilibrium in which all are fulfilled in each other and each can enjoy all (a creative kingdom of love) then there must be a power at work which will absorb powerful power rather than counter power with power.

David Jenkins' words are a salutary warning to those Christians who propose to do right by violence. However, he does not say how the structures are to be changed. This is where Max Kohnstamm is most helpful. At Geneva 1966 he talked about the peaceful way in which Christians can help to change the obsolete structures. He talked about cracks appearing in the structures and sowing seeds in the cracks. What he had in mind was what has often happened in past history. The structures within which people have lived have at times become inadequate. For instance, after the mediaeval period the faults in the feudal and other systems appeared as large cracks. The church pointed to the faults and helped new structures to appear. So now it is the task of the church to point to the obvious cracks and so help people to accept the structures needed for healthy human life. This means patiently waiting for the right moment and courage to act when the time is ripe. This is the peaceful way, not the way of violence.[16]

NOTES

1. See E. de Vries, *Man in Rapid Social Change.*
2. See John Kenneth Galbraith, *The New Industrial State,* and *The Affluent Society.*
3. In an article appearing in 'ISAL Documentation', a publication of the Movement on Church and Society in Latin America, January 1969, and quoted in *Risk,* Vol. 6, No. 2, 1969, pp. 40, 41.
4. See 'Development', *Risk,* Vol. 5, No. 2, 1969, p. 42.
5. Art. cit., p. 36, quoted from Pope Paul VI's address in Bogota.
6. Art. cit., p. 41.
7. See J. A. T. Robinson, *Christian Freedom in a Permissive Society,* SCM Press 1970, pp. 1ff.
8. WCC Studies No. 8, 1970.
9. See the *Journal of Peace Research,* No. 2, 1969, p. 13a, Takeshi Ishida's article 'Beyond the Traditional Concept of Peace in Different Cultures'.
10. See *Conflict, Violence and Peace,* p. 141.
11. See Address by Chairman of WCC Central Committee at Addis Ababa quoted in *This Month,* EPS, Jan. 1971.
12. See *Conflict, Violence and Peace,* pp. 87ff.
13. See B. H. Liddell-Hart, *Strategy – the Indirect Approach,* Faber 1954.
14. See *Study Encounter,* Vol. VI, No. 3, 1970.
15. See *In Search of a Theology of Development,* SODEPAX 1970, pp. 51, 52.
16. See my *Wealth, Peace and Godliness,* ch. 5.

4

New Masters, Old Servants - Politics

Politics deals with the art of governing a nation. In a modern democratic state it deals with the machinery and mechanics whereby the purposes of government are achieved, such as the security, freedom and welfare of the members of the nation. It provides for the election of those who will form the government, for their replacement and for the rules and procedures under which they will operate. Politics also, however, deals with the structures within which the government of a nation operates. These structures vary from the Athenian city state of classical times to the dictatorship of more recent times and include the parliamentary democratic systems to which we have become accustomed. From time to time these political arrangements are found to be inadequate and changes have to be made to meet new situations.

One of these was the colonial system of government whereby a country or a geographical area was governed by decisions made outside by a colonial power. The need to change from a colonial structure of government to one which implements decisions made by the people themselves largely arose because the colonial system did not serve the interests of the colonial peoples.

This is what the Afro-Asian countries decided when they met at Bandung in 1955. The arrangement whereby their countries were governed by political decisions made by colonial powers, was named as the primary cause of their underdevelopment. A new system should be demanded. These countries should become independent and governed by decisions made by themselves within their own countries. This was where the demand for political independence was first articulated by the colonial people.

It is difficult for those outside ex-colonial territories to appreciate the strong feelings which are entertained, particularly in intellectual circles, about colonialism. The following quotations are typical of those who make political and cultural judgments on colonialism. It is not our intention to assess them but simply to let them convey these feelings.

Writing in a preparatory volume for the Geneva Conference in 1966, *Responsible Government in a Revolutionary Age*, Richard Andriamanjato, a Christian pastor and politician from Madagascar, states:

> Colonialism was an external factor added to, and possibly imposed upon, the conflicts and divergencies that already existed. It took little account of the human dignity of the black man and was interested only in exploitation, sources of income and all that could be converted into cash or exported, thus enriching the colonizing country. . . . The occupation and division of Africa were conceived, at best, with a view to the prosperity of European trade. Even the attack on slavery was included for the purpose of improving the long-term consequences of what could justly be called the wholesale exploitation of Africa; and the division and distribution of spheres of influence were based simply on money-making self-interest.[1]

He adds:

> The colonial powers made a concerted effort to destroy all aspects of culture and to eradicate all sense of membership within the human family. In short, they tried to inculcate into the African consciousness a principle of discrimination that put the white man on a superior plane ... This destruction of traditional authority and culture sought only to uproot the African from his physical and sociological environment and to reduce him to a mere cog in the machine designed for production and exploitation.

Aimé Cesaire has something to say about this in his *Discours sur le Colonialisme*[2] where he says of colonialism:

> The decisive motive here is that of the adventurer and the pirate, of the wholesale grocer and the privateer, of the gold prospector and the trader, of greed and force, while behind them is thrown the evil shadow of a form of civilization which at any moment in its history finds itself compelled from within to extend on to a world scale the competition between its conflicting economies ... In the relationship between colonizer and colonized there is room only for forced labour, intimidation, press-ganging, police, taxation, robbery, violation, compulsory breeding, scorn, suspicious arrogance, conceit, insensitivity.

Others have expressed the same sentiments, including Sekou Touré, the President of Guinea, and Franz Fanon who says that it is necessary to root out every trace of colonialism in order to recover self-respect: 'It is necessary to question the whole colonial situation.'[3]

At the time of Bandung there was considerable debate as to whether political independence should be granted before certain conditions had been satisfied. One of these was the availability of sufficient administrative and political expertise within these countries. Accordingly, under the French colonial system a preparation for independence was launched in 1956 with the *loi-cadre* (constitutional framework) which was to give the native people a greater share in administration. It allowed a period of apprenticeship in power. In the British colonies greater responsibility was delegated in varying stages up to internal self-government, the last step before full independence.

However, the centre of the debate was on the economic viability of the territories which were demanding independence and the question canvassed was whether political independence should not be the consequence of economic performance rather than its condition. The argument which weighed with the colonies in favour of political independence before economic viability was that economic growth depended largely on political decisions, and until they were responsible for their own destiny the local effort and initiative would lack the encouragement necessary to economic growth. For this and other reasons political independence was demanded irrespective of economic performance.

The theme of this chapter is the political disillusion which has followed this necessary basic choice. It will attempt to describe some of the causes of the political disappointment and some of the solutions which are being proposed. It does not set out to criticize the choice which the new nations made in favour of political independence in spite of economic difficulties. This choice was inevitable. It was right. But just as economic growth has not been sufficient to satisfy the needs of people in developing countries, so political independence in the service of economic growth has not supplied them with the freedom and justice for which the original choice opted. The title is designed to convey this message.

The fault lies not so much with the political leaders. Their intentions were good and many of them were highly sensitive to political realities from the beginning. The fault lies in the world economic and political imbalances which colonialism had helped to create. The nations emerging from colonialism had been particularly affected by the years during which they had been under foreign rule. Not only had their economies been determined by the needs of western industrial society which took away their raw products for processing in the factories of these more advanced countries. They had also by these very means helped to put these countries in such an industrially advantageous position that they themselves could never hope to compete with them in trade on the world market.

The period of dependence had, moreover, deprived them of the initiative which is essential to the assertion of viable independence. They had in many places, particularly in Africa, been discouraged from regarding themselves as any better than second class citizens. This had bred an inferiority complex with inevitable effects on their response to the challenges of independence. In India the caste system, though not due to colonialism itself, had created a psychological situation where the outcaste had an inbuilt diffidence about his own ability to participate in any of the social and economic efforts required by independence, while those belonging to the *élite* groups found it equally difficult to accept the outcastes as equals in the new political era.

The cultural effects of colonialism had created another kind of diffidence about themselves among the people of the dependent territories. Western techniques and ideas had been so effective in these places that the local culture became a debased currency. The value systems came to be related to western culture and it was these which became the standards of assessment and the goals of achievement. It is difficult for a westerner to estimate the effects of cultural devaluation. He is not likely to succeed in understanding it until he finds his own culture being flouted and debased by those who do not understand it. Then he may understand what has really happened to colonial people through insensitivity to their culture.

It was in a situation such as this that the political leaders of the countries which opted for independence at Bandung in 1955 tried to make independence viable. Unlike western nations they started without any national identity as an original base from which to work. African leaders represented little more than tribal groups and areas which had not been integrated into conscious political units. Even India did not have a national identity to compare with a European nation. Indonesia was still a collection of islands united only in the mind of Sukarno, without any real political unification except Dutch rule. The Caribbean islands were still feeling their way towards an identity. Inhibited by economic realities which placed effective power outside their boundaries, and governed from the Colonial Office, they were still a long way off from nationhood. In Latin America the *caudillo* mentality and the inherited system of government and land tenure placed severe restrictions on their title to description as modern nations which exist for the sake of the people.

This brief description helps us to understand the tremendous task which faced the political leaders of the emerging nations as they attempted the venture of independence. There were four basic needs

which the politicians had to supply to enable this task to be successfully undertaken. The attempt to supply them has exposed issues
which still need to be faced and which, in many cases, cannot be
resolved from the political base from which these developing countries have started as separate entities.

The first need was to establish nation-states. European history
supplied an analogy for the politicians for their own situation. Many
of them, in fact, had been educated in western universities during
the colonial period, and most of them had been introduced to
European history and political ideas through the education system
supplied for them by the colonial powers. They saw that just as
European nations during the fifteenth and sixteenth centuries
developed their national identity through which they became powerful states, so also those geographic areas in the new world which
were in a similar pre-political state, would have to be moulded
into nations.

They were faced also with problems similar to the emerging
nation states of the first mediaeval period in Europe. Tribalism in
many parts of Africa formed the boundary of allegiance and
authority. To weld tribes into a nation in any area previously
governed by the colonial power was itself an immense task and
presented formidable problems. Tribal hatreds and animosities had
to be surmounted. On the other hand, the detribalization which had
been caused by colonial exploitation had, according to African
scholars, tended to remove those allegiances and disciplines which
were necessary to build up a nation. Andriamanjato again writes:

> The fundamental unity which forms the basis of the individual
> consciousness, tribal or popular, and which is rooted in a form
> of civilization that people have been obliged for some time to
> judge with greater objectivity, has been broken. It has been
> replaced by one sole condition – that of the victim of colonialism,
> of a man without dignity, without will, without direct respon-
> sibility, of a man who is a mere tool or instrument. It is certainly
> difficult to see how a mass of individuals living in a particular
> part of the world are to be welded into an organized unity of a
> state when they have not the slightest consciousness of any wider
> unity – racial, national, tribal, cultural, historical or geographical.
> It was a matter of discovering some centre of common interest.[4]

When the task of fighting the colonial power, the common enemy,
had passed with independence, the sole unifying factor was lost and
fragmentation was threatened as has been so clearly demonstrated
in the recent Nigerian civil war.

Usually the new independent countries followed the geographic
demarcation left by colonial occupation and agreed upon between

the powers at various times by negotiation or treaty. Indonesia, which consists of a large number of islands over an area of 3,000 miles long and 1,100 miles wide with a land space of 738,865 square miles, was not unified until the arrival of the Dutch in the late fifteenth century. There had been empires there in preceding centuries from time to time, but it was the colonial period which imposed unified rule over the area which is now known as Indonesia. With the departure of the Dutch, first in 1941 and, after the reoccupation, again in 1949, the task of welding this area into a nation was undertaken by Sukarno and Hatta.

Nor did the Dutch colonial rule weld the Indonesian peoples into a nation. Unity was emphatically not its goal. On the contrary, until the end it could conceive of Indonesia only as a colony to which was applied the classic colonial principle of 'divide and rule'.[5]

Their task can be estimated from the fact that there are 3,000 islands, inhabited by Javanese, Sundanese, Balinese, Dayaks, Taradjas, Malays, and a host of later immigrant groups with a diversity of languages, dialects and religions, shared by about a hundred million people.

The task of nation-building in situations such as these, which are characteristic of the emerging nations of the world, has been carried out along a fairly consistent pattern which has produced similar problems everywhere. The way this has been done has been to discover some experience, interest or other factor, which would be accepted as common to the whole population and by which they would be given a distinctive identity. Very often this contained a large element of myth, but generally this gave it its cohesive power. Sukarno spoke of Indonesianness. In the Caribbean, where a new attempt is being made to bring the people of the region together, the emphasis is on the common experience of slavery which, however, tends to exclude the non-black people. Generally, it is the name of the new nation which is the rallying point and anti-colonialism provides the emotions with the aggressiveness required for the task of nation-building.

The general effect of the normal pattern of nation-building has been to emphasize the new political units as self-conscious nations with exclusive interests. For the most part, therefore, it has been impossible to engage in the task of nation-building without the use of nationalism. This has raised the whole issue of nationalism in modern political development. In particular it has raised the question of the value of national identity in the modern world where political and economic realities are requiring the formation of larger groupings for the sake of efficiency and security. The problem is whether the emphasis of the emerging nations on their national identity, with its corollary of nationalism, can be correlated with the need for regionalism in the sense of national and economic collectives. This leads us to a brief consideration of nationalism as an instrument of nation-building in the context of modern development.

Nationalism is an ambiguous term and it is necessary to distinguish the various meanings which are attached to it in order to avoid emotive judgments about what has great potential for good and evil. Nationalism can have at least three different meanings. It may refer to democratic nationalism. In this sense it is an expression of the view that political authority belongs to the people who compose the nation. This is the sense in which nationalism was expressed during the French Revolution, where it can be described as revolutionary nationalism because it opposed the conception that authority belongs to the monarchy by divine right. Implicit in this view is the belief that the nation is not constituted by nature or by divine right, but by the human volition of the people who assent to it or create it. Democratic nationalism emphasizes the will of the people in the creation and maintenance of the nation and adherence to it. It means that a person born in another country, speaking another language, may belong to a nation provided he exercises his will to do so.

Opposed to democratic nationalism is territorial nationalism. According to this doctrine the native land or soil, rather than the individual will, is primary in the creation of a nation. The emphasis is upon the land, the culture, the tradition, the language and religion to which the individual member of the nation belongs. It forms the theme of poetry and song and romantic literature. Its emotional appeal is very strong and arises out of the cultural roots which people have in the tradition and history of their country as well as the protection they derive from belonging to a collective with similar roots. Through it people derive or maintain a significance which appears to be necessary to their personal nature.

The third type of nationalism is that which is rooted in the sense of superiority of a nation or the basic group within it. This is similar to territorial nationalism in that it is rooted in culture or race or land or religion. But it is different in the sense that it regards itself as superior to all others. From this is derived its usual claim to be the 'chosen nation'. Nazi nationalism was of this kind which emphasized the superiority of the German people. It has tremendous development potential but at the same time, it is essentially restrictive. It leads to imperialism and to jingoism, and the idea 'my country right or wrong'.

In discussing nationalism it is important to keep in mind the fact that these meanings and variations of them have to be distinguished in any given situation. This is particularly important in the development era, since nationalism can have both a positive creative, and a negative destructive, role to play. This needs to be remembered because in the development debate, the nationalism of developing countries is frequently criticized by economists, political thinkers and theologians in the developed countries. It is generally criticized, however, on the assumption that it has become an ideology like Nazism. Whenever nationalism of this kind occurs its fault is too obvious to need further comment. But all nationalism is not of this kind; nor is this the kind usually found in the developing countries. In those countries it is not an expression of the superiority of their race or culture, but of their equality with those of the developed world.

Moreover, economists and political theorists who emphasize the importance of political and economic integration on a regional and world basis, must recognize the need which nationalism in the right sense of the word serves for the emerging nations at this stage of development. National sovereignty is the sole guarantee which they have against exploitation and discrimination until proper safeguards are provided. This is the reason why British Honduras turned down the Seventeen Proposals of Senator Webster for independence in 1969. It limited national sovereignty.

On the other hand, Henri Burgelin, writing from the point of view of the developed West, says:

The mastery of new technology implies increased international co-operation. For a long time to come, for example, no African state will be able to furnish alone the financial, technological and scientific means needed to establish an atomic industry. A pooling of the resources of each, and co-operation with countries that are economically more highly developed are indispensable to the transformations required by the situation in Africa; but pooling and co-operation of that kind are possible only in an atmosphere of order and peace – and this would be destroyed by the constitution and strengthening of national states ... It seemed to us that the national state belonged to a certain age, a particular stage in the economic development of the West, but that this stage is over and is not indispensable for those countries that are developing today. On the contrary, the nationalism implied in this type of state is a factor, even for the underdeveloped countries, that contributes to stagnation and economic underdevelopment. At the political level, its disadvantages are considerable, and nothing justifies them unless they are imposed by economic necessity.[6]

This provokes the simple question: Will the developed countries also surrender their sovereignty? What guarantees are provided to safeguard, not only the economic needs, but also the other values which make up human life in the developing countries? At this time in history, there seems to most observers to be no realistic alternative to nationalism in the best sense of the term for the developing countries, but it must be one which is prepared for the limitations which the process of development demands from time to time.

The second basic need which the leaders of the developing countries had to face at the time of independence was democratization. The stage of political development which they inherited varied a great deal, from the British colonial model, which had already begun to encourage the political participation of the people, to those places where direct rule had been exercised by the imperial power without any attempt to share decisions with the people themselves. The picture we are looking at, therefore, is varied and to do justice to it we should have to examine each situation separately. As this is impossible here, we have to be content with generalizations.

After independence the new nation states required a system of government that would enable them to provide the conditions conducive to the attainment of those ends which were accepted as desirable. These were the welfare, dignity and liberty of the individual member of the state. The obvious method of government was, therefore, democracy, in which each citizen was able to exercise his power of choice through the vote. For this reason the invariable policy was to establish democratic institutions of government in the new emerging nations.

The task of providing these democratic institutions, however, proved to be very problematic and varied from place to place. The claims of strong government in the interests of order often conflicted with the demands of individual and group freedom, resulting either in the use of coercive measures by the government, which then tended to become less democratic, or in an inefficient economic and social system.

The main reason for the problems of democratic government was that neither had the people always been prepared by education for democracy, nor had the society in which they were now democratic citizens been integrated sufficiently to remove those tensions which could only be checked by coercive force. For instance, what A. D. Lindsay says of the English was hardly true of many of the new nations ten years ago:

England's social conformity is the spontaneous achievement of individuals. The individual has been socialized in such a measure that in all essential manifestations he spontaneously reacts to society and the interests maintaining it ... The Englishman's dictator is installed in his heart. Authority does not need to put him in leading strings because it can depend on his using his freedom only to the extent that society can bear.[7]

In India and Africa, the same voluntary and spontaneous reaction to society and the interests maintaining it, was not available. The primordial sentiments and attachments of people based on race, religion, region, tribe, language, were too strong to allow them to surrender them easily in the interests of civil order. Even of India it is said:

Primordial discontent often expresses itself in India in such extreme and unconstitutional forms as burning the national flag and copies of the constitution, and in demanding the division of the country into several independent states. In such a situation, when people are unwilling to respond spontaneously to the demands of national integration, government has to move them towards unity by force or mass psychology or a mixture between the two ... A positive and powerful government is needed in India not only for maintaining the unity and integrity of the nation, but to enable the individual citizen to enjoy all those fundamental rights and liberties that are granted and guaranteed to him by the constitution. Democracy in India has to struggle against a background of an apolitical tradition, political indifference and ignorance and civic unconsciousness. Dynasties came to power and perished, empires rose and fell, yet the common man was blissfully ignorant of all these changes. Such political apathy and indifference, though understandable in a monarchy or an oligarchy, expose democracy to the encroachments of dictatorship and totalitarian regimes.[8]

The absence of democratic disciplines has, therefore, been a great handicap in these neo-democratic countries, and in particular in their efforts to create economic growth. In so far as an economy depends on certain attitudes and these in turn on the social and political context in which people live, a democracy is particularly vulnerable economically where this context has not been created. It is this need to provide the means of economic growth which, as much as any other factor, has caused several of the new nations either to modify their democracy or to use oppressive measures.

Modifications of the democratic system have taken different forms in different places. The most common is the one-party system of government, whereby free elections are held to choose a government. In effect, it generally means that the people have an opportunity to register their objection to a party or a politician but not

to elect an alternative. But there are variations. The best known of
these are those of some of the African states where the variation
extends from that which is centred upon a personality cult to that
centred on an ideology, though the difference is not always immediately obvious. President Nkrumah, when he was head of the Ghana
state wrote:

> The Convention People's Party is Ghana and Ghana is the Con-
> vention People's Party. There are some people, both staff and
> students (of the University College of Ghana), who mistakenly
> believe that the words 'academic freedom' carry with them a
> spirit of hostility to our Party and Government ... The Conven-
> tion People's Party cannot allow this confusion of academic
> freedom with disloyalty and anti-government bias.

The ghost of the old masters appears in the new rulers.

Even in areas where full democratic processes are used along
the British pattern, there is a tendency for governments to emphasize
the economic at the expense of the social needs of the country. The
argument is that it is necessary to provide a stable, strong government in order to attract investment. Strong government sometimes
means repression of any form of demonstration against inequalities
and injustices. In the Caribbean, where the form of economic
development has been structured by external investment, the growing gap between the rich and the poor has set off a number of
demonstrations, some amounting to riotous conduct, for instance in
Curaçao and particularly in Trinidad. Some of these have been
associated with the USA initiated black-power movement, mainly
because the underprivileged sector of the community are the black
people. It is usual in these situations for the government to be
accused of being oppressive and to use police brutality to suppress
any form of anti-government action. Because of the economic
struggle which demands 'strong' government, the new masters are
coming under severe criticism from the old servants.

This is what occurs in several countries where liberal democracy
is constitutionally established. In others different forms of democracy have had to be instituted to meet the lack of the necessary
disciplines and to accommodate the stage of political development
reached. The best known of these, apart from the people's democratic dictatorship system followed in the communist countries,
which somewhat stretches the meaning we normally give to
democracy, is the 'basic democracy' of Pakistan, which is designed
to accommodate the political situation in that country with its
Mohammedan background and give the people the power to decide
its own destiny. Then there is the 'guided democracy' of Indonesia.

The 'guided democracy' of President Sukarno was instituted in 1959. It

provided for a cabinet responsible to the President, a parliament in which elected members were supplemented by presidentially appointed members, and a Provisional People's Consultative Council, appointed by the President and vested with power to determine the general direction and policy of the state. The President carried the mandate of this body and assumed the office of Prime Minister, his cabinet being led by several Deputy Prime Ministers.[9]

This was based on a constitution which incorporated the Pantja Sila, or Five Principles – Belief in God, Nationalism, Humanitarianism (sometimes called Internationalism), the People's Sovereignty, and Social Justice. There appears to be more guidance than democracy in this set up and it clearly depended on the personality of Sukarno himself who replaced the Dutch masters.

Even one of the most enlightened approaches to the establishment of democracy of the liberal parliamentary kind has recently been under strain. It is that of Dr Eric Williams of Trinidad. Himself an economist and political scientist of considerable academic standing, he came to power at the head of the People's National Movement in 1956 as the result of a programme of public political education. At regular intervals Dr Williams would lecture crowds amounting to over ten thousand people in what he called 'The University of Woodford Square', which is an open-air park in Port-of-Spain. There he explained political and economic issues which lay behind the decisions which the government needed to make, and an enlightened political consciousness grew in Port-of-Spain to enable democratic processes to be followed. Yet in 1970, there was an attempt at an armed rebellion which nearly succeeded in overthrowing the government because of economic difficulties felt by the workers.

There are also the serious questions which have been raised about the compatibility of liberal parliamentary democracy with modern economic needs, and whether the attempt in the emerging nations of the world to establish democracies on a parliamentary basis will prove viable.

André Philip[10] has remarked on the irony of the developing countries' efforts in this direction. He says that the enterprise is contrary to economic and political realities which demand larger groupings and decisions at the economic and technological level as prerequisites to any political action. He says that developing countries are in the same position as Europe in the fifteenth, sixteenth and seventeenth centuries when nation states were being created.

They talk, he says, about a utopian revolution through political change, whereas in Europe the revolution is already taking place under the influence of technological advance. What is being done is that decisions are being made within that revolution with the intention of guiding it. These decisions are being made not by politicians but by those who formulate the development plan, at local and regional level. It is only after these decisions have been taken with extensive participation at the technical and popular level that the plan is finally ratified. Speaking, of course, out of the experience of France where this process has produced remarkable change in the past fifteen years, André Philip thinks this is the direction in which political organization is going. Parliamentary democracy is giving way to industrial participatory democracy. In the developing countries politicians continue to think and act differently. They still try to control the course of development without the competence to understand the technical issues involved. Political interference with industrial development either at the point of planning and initiation, or subsequently, is to subordinate efficiency to political ends, and in effect to allow individual pressures to be exercised in the interests of political power. When efficiency is subordinated to votes, healthy development cannot be guaranteed. This is the implication of André Philip's analysis.

The third issue which faced those who undertook the political task, particularly in the East, was the secularization of their sacral and religious societies. As distinct from secularism, which is an ideology, secularization is the process whereby historical and physical events are increasingly explained as the effects of natural causes, and policies and programmes are determined by reference exclusively to such causes. Religious sanctions are consequently reduced and replaced by values and criteria which are tangible and non-religious in developing countries. Secularization is the process that accompanies the modernization which most political leaders, observing its effect in the West, have desired for their own societies. Based as it is on the scientific explanation of things, modernization puts the results of scientific investigation into effect in the form of technology and industrialization. It is as a result of this that secularization takes place.

There are two causes of secularization. The first is the need to modernize and industrialize a society. When this is done the secular process follows of its own accord. The sacral basis of primitive societies, along with their culture and ethics derived from religious sanctions, begins to disintegrate as a result of the need to introduce industrial disciplines. Communities bound together by a sacral culture break up and behaviour begins to be determined by new sanctions which accommodate the needs of modernization. The moral and psychological problems raised by modernization and the urbanization which follows it, of course, create issues for those responsible for the political life of developing countries. But we shall not discuss these here.

It is the second cause of secularization which is more immediately relevant to the political field with which we are now dealing. This is when secularization is adopted as a deliberate social policy in the interests of political ends. It has been found to be necessary to follow a deliberate policy of secularization in many of the developing countries, especially in Asia and Africa, in order not only to meet the needs of industrial modernization but also to provide a sound basis for political community. The sacral basis of society which was suitable to the integration of a tribal group in Africa and gave support to the caste system in Hindu India, could not integrate a nation which consisted of several tribes and several religious groups. Almost invariably some measure of secularization had to be adopted to provide a common ground on which to unite the emerging nation.

Secularization, in this sense, did not necessarily mean a repudiation of religion or of belief in God. It meant that the culture of a particular religion ceased to be the foundation on which the new nation was founded. Instead the secular principle itself became the basis on which religious groups and sacral systems were contained within the nation. In fact, pluralism which could not be contained by an exclusive religious foundation became a possibility in a secular state.

Several of those nations, therefore, which began with a particular religious foundation, found that they had to modify their constitution in order to accommodate minorities within the nation by accepting some form of secular basis. Pakistan began as an Islamic Republic in 1947. However, the description of the state as such was abandoned in the revised constitution after the military *coup* in 1958 and no attempt has been made to prescribe Islamic tradition since that time.[11]

Similarly, Indonesia, which is predominantly Muslim, has had to accept a secular constitution in the interests of national integration. For apart from the large Muslim population there is a strong and growing Batak Christian Church as well as other minority religious groups which could not be contained, or at least could not be encouraged, in a Muslim state. Notwithstanding the first of the Pantja Sila or Five Principles, on which the constitution of Indonesia is based, belief in God, the state is secular, since it is not committed to any particular religion.

There are still some states, however, which have retained their religious basis in Asia, such as Thailand, Cambodia and Laos, but these are exceptions to the rule. In fact, following Mexico and Turkey, and before them France, it is on a secular basis that the new countries are founded. With the exception of China, the most important example of these is India, which is officially secular. Its constitution pledges its governments to give no privileges to any religious body. The Republic of India prohibited all discrimination on grounds of religion, race or caste in its constitution in 1950 and in fact this predominantly Hindu country elected a Muslim President as the head of its secular state in 1967.[12]

However, secularization has posed many critical problems in those countries with traditional religious cultures. It is true that except for those countries which have taken an anti-clerical and an anti-religious stand as, for instance, China and the Soviet Union, the new nations have not renounced religion in the sense of belief in God, and some have even accepted a particular religion officially, as in the case of Pakistan. Nevertheless, the political constitutions of the new nations struck at the roots of those religions which were bound up with their culture. This is also true of those religions which prescribed laws and practices, such as the Muslim faith.

David L. Edwards in his book *Religion and Change*,[13] describes the dilemma of Islam when it was faced with the changes caused by westernization and new political arrangements in Africa and the East. He says:

No other Islamic country has undergone changes as drastic as Turkey, partly because no other country is geographically so suitable to westernization ... But in parts of Islam there already exists an intelligentsia moulded by an education which is western in its ethos; the development of technology extends western influences more subtly, and western popular culture seeps through. It is possible to prophesy that other situations will develop towards an explosion or slow erosion which will do at least as much damage as was done in Turkey to the traditional fabric of Islam, unless Islam can reform itself voluntarily. And 'Islam reformed ... is Islam no longer'.

David Edwards explains that this is because Islamic society was the personal creation of the prophet Muhammed, who founded a single community both political and religious, 'armed with the scimitar as well as with faith'. As distinct from Jesus who lived in a closely controlled political world to which he could not legislate, Muhammed entered a social vacuum in Arabia and met little resistance in his westward march. He was thus involved in creating a new civilization through his militant religious faith which laid down the rules under which Muslim societies must be governed and prescribed the details of social and personal life. Secularization is a deadly blow to Islam because it challenges it at a point where it is particularly vulnerable, namely, its political and social application. For this is precisely what secularization means in this context; the removal of social and political life from the control of a religious culture and ethic.

Christianity, on the other hand, is not vulnerable at this point in the same way as Islam. For the kingdom of Christ 'is not of this world', and it does not prescribe the political and social regulations under which people must live. It is true that Christendom was an attempt to translate Christianity into social and cultural terms, but the collapse of the medieval experiment has not destroyed the Christian faith itself. It has simply revealed the contingent nature of all attempts to express Christianity in a particular cultural form. Not so with Islam which is fundamentally a religion expressed in a particular form.

In fact, Christianity, as distinct from Islam, is compatible with a secular state. Christianity does not necessarily prescribe secularization nor, indeed, does it forbid a sacred society as some secularizers have implied. Christianity can live within a secular state without violence to its essential nature. More than that there are circumstances where Christianity's concern for human welfare and the political and social structures which are likely to ensure this, will compel Christians to promote secularization in order to free men from bonds which are directly or indirectly made by sacral religions.

This is the reason why certain Christians in India have been active in promoting the secular state of Pandit Nehru. Hinduism does not provide, so they believe, the basis on which a democratic state can be built up in India, nor a means whereby the plural society now coming into being can be integrated. Devanandan, and now M. M. Thomas, have been the leading Indian Christians who have assisted in the secularization of Indian society through the studies which they have published from the Christian Institute in Bangalore.[14] In fact, some of their studies have become required reading for civil servants in some of the Indian states.

Yet secularization has become problematic also for Christianity, which gave it birth. As it grows out of its first Christian clothes and asserts its freedom from the ethics of the family which fostered it, it is liberating people for new forms of bondage and taking ultimate meaning out of life. As Lesslie Newbigin says in his book *Honest Religion for Secular Man*,[15] in which he discusses the conditions without which a secular society cannot achieve the ends for which it is promoted:

Specifically I suggest that if the mastery which is given to man through the process of secularization is not held within the context of man's responsibility to God, the result will be a new slavery; that if the dynamism of 'development', the drive to a new kind of human society, is not informed by the biblical faith concerning the nature of the kingdom of God, it will end in totalitarianism; and that if the secular critique of all established orders is not informed and directed by the knowledge of God, it will end in self-destructive nihilism.

This sums up the causes of the secular disappointment of the political ambition.

NOTES

1. Op. cit., article, 'Nation Building in a Post-Colonial World', p. 131.
2. Présence Africaine, Paris, 3rd ed. 1958.
3. *The Wretched of the Earth.*
4. Art. cit., p. 136.
5. See Frank I. Cooley, *Indonesia: Church and Society*, p. 21.
6. See *Responsible Government in a Revolutionary Age*, p. 275.
7. Quoted in *Responsible Government in a Revolutionary Age*, p. 221.
8. Quoted in *Responsible Government in a Revolutionary Age*, pp. 203, 207.
9. See *Indonesia*, p. 24.
10. See *Responsible Government in a Revolutionary Age*, article by André Philip on 'The Revolutionary Change in the Structure of European Economic Life', p. 115.
11. See Leonard Binder, *Religion and Politics in Pakistan*, Berkeley 1961.
12. See D. Eugene Smith, *India as a Secular State*.
13. Hodder & Stoughton 1969, pp. 77ff.
14. See P. D. Devanandan and M. M. Thomas, *Christian Participation in Nation Building in India*, and M. M. Thomas, *The Christian Response to the Asian Revolution*.
15. Pp. 30ff.

5

Who Decides? - Neo-colonialism

A cartoon in World Christian Education shows a man laboriously climbing a ladder. Above him is another man who rests his foot on his head. At the same time he stretches his hand down to help him up the ladder. The helping hand is designed to suggest the aid which the developed give to the developing countries. The foot which presses the man down signifies the structures of trade and aid which prevent the poorer countries catching up the advanced industrialized nations. It is a cartoon about what is known in the Third World as 'neo-colonialism'. John Karefa Smart puts it in this way:

> The danger of what has loosely been termed 'neo-colonialism' is very real. This embraces every attempt, overt or otherwise, to bring the new nation under some form or other of political attachment to the previous colonial rulers.[1]

This quotation introduces us to an interpretation common in developing countries of the general feeling of frustration felt in post-colonial territories after they had experimented with their political independence for only a few years. By neo-colonialism they mean that the old colonial shackles have been put back on them again in a new form, and independence is little better than a political deception. Let us examine this interpretation of the causes of disillusion with development.

If we cannot examine what is described as 'every attempt' to recreate the political attachment of the new nations to the ex-colonial rulers, we can look at some of those which have been alleged during this period. According to the neo-colonial theory, they are all operated by the simple device of replacing the old direct administrative controls with new types of control. When these new controls are put on they remove initiative, responsibility, and the possibility of making reliable local decisions from the hands of the new nations and they place them in the hands of people outside. The neo-colonial theory says that whatever the appearance may be, the real power is in the hands of other people, and not of those whose destiny is being determined. This is done by manipulating the systems of control so that vital decisions are made outside.

One particular complaint coming from the developing countries is that the new nations are so dependent in certain respects on external forces for development that they are unable to determine effectively the pattern which is most suited to their needs. The way in which their economy, and in turn their politics, society and culture, is shaped is decided by external forces and not by internal decisions. Lately, the developing countries have even begun to criticize the churches. For instance, studies made of development by the churches are accused of representing the point of view of those outside :

> The Beirut approach seems to us to be largely from the point of view of developed countries. The voice of the younger churches does not seem to have been effective enough for want of suitable and adequate representation. The Church in this report is committing the same mistake as aiding governments; looking at the problems of development through their own eyes. If the Church is to be true to its convictions then it must listen to the views of those in developing countries for adopting a suitable development strategy.[2]

This transfer of control in turn has had effects on the initiative of the poor countries. They started out on the independence venture expecting and determined to use their own initiative. It was they themselves who would formulate the plans for their own future. There would be no interference when the colonial administrators had left. They entered the new era inspired by the feeling that everything was now in their own hands and that they could create their own future. Instead, they claim that when they formulated their plans, often after intensive research, these had to be changed to suit arrangements made elsewhere. They had to invite other people, experts from the developed countries, to come in and advise. They found that the advice suited the convenience of the country from which the advisers came and seldom did they see matters from the point of view of the new nation. So the initiative passed out of the hands of the poor countries.

In turn this has had an effect on their sense of responsibility. Continual frustration of their ideas, plans and efforts has had the inevitable consequence of making people in the developing countries feel that they do not really have the power to make decisions which will work. Their sense of responsibility for what happens is being gradually eroded and a fatalism is creeping back causing a paralysis in many sectors of the community. When they have failed to implement their own plans, they claim that they have to accept new commitments on the basis of external advice and promises. Dependent on this advice and assistance, they say that the last word is not really theirs. This kind of situation drains away that sense of responsibility which is essential to development. This is the sad and pathetic picture of the disillusion of the facile hopes which developing countries once entertained.

This is what they mean by 'neo-colonialism'. For them it means loss of effective control, reduction of initiative and a fatalistic paralysis in many sectors of the community. This encourages the continuance of paternalistic attitudes on the one side, and a dependent begging mentality on the other. These are the attitudes of colonialism. The relationship which creates them is not military and administrative control, but economic power. Neo-colonialism is, therefore, interpreted as the manipulation of economic forces by the ex-colonial powers in order to continue the dependence of the new nations in new forms for the benefit of the richer nations. John Karefa Smart puts it in these words:

> In addition to its political application, the concept of 'neo-colonialism' also includes all forms of economic relationship that place the newly independent nation in a position of dependence for the continued exploitation of its resources and for general economic development. Such neo-colonialist economic power may arise through financial loans or through subsidiary industrial or commercial corporations, which, although they may be registered in the new nation and under its laws, are, nevertheless, owned and directed by a parent company in the previously metropolitan country.
>
> Another important neo-colonialist phenomenon is the creation of associations whose aim is to control the external market for the raw materials and natural and mineral resources of the former colony, which at the same time, continues to be a ready-made market for the manufactured goods from the metropolitan country. Although some benefit will accrue to the newly independent state, the major financial and economic advantages lie with the controlling groups abroad.[3]

In her book *The Barrel of a Gun*, Ruth First describes the way in which industrial empires are built in Africa by large western corporations. She gives examples of this new colonialism by which the West is establishing a stranglehold on the struggling African states, and how the great industrial corporations are able to manoeuvre this operation. What we are being told is that it is through the economic ties of dependence, woven by industrial relationships between the rich and poor countries, that the new empires are being built up in the Third World.

Economic dependence has already been discussed in relation to investment.[4] We have already seen how investment patterns are dictated by the external investing corporation, and how these patterns impose domination and dependence upon the developing countries. What we have in mind, of course, is private investment, which must be kept distinct from official aid which refers to the direct grants and loans made bilaterally by developed to developing nations or multilaterally by international agencies on behalf of the richer nations.

It can be argued that private investment in developing countries does not raise any neo-colonial issues because it is entirely a business transaction. The investing corporation has a responsibility to the shareholders and its responsibility to the country where the investment is made exists only in so far as good relations and the economic climate are affected by the behaviour of the company in that country. A business corporation cannot be treated as a charity organization operating for the benefit of the developing country where it invests its capital. It can equally be argued that the corporation does not dictate the terms of investment, but simply negotiates them with the local authorities who have the power to reject their proposals. Or again, it can with the same plausibility be said that unless the poor countries get foreign capital and expertise, development cannot be accelerated and that it is a means of bringing considerable revenue to the country through wages earned by local labour and services provided by local industries.

On the other hand, the developing countries claim that there are other considerations. Principally there are the moral considerations which are raised by the fact that much of the wealth invested in the developing countries was originally acquired by the investors through the exploitation of the resources of these countries during the colonial regime. Even after due weight has been given to the cost paid by the colonizers to acquire this wealth in terms of risk, labour and expenditure of money and skill, they claim that unpaid debts still remain in the overall balance sheet. The transactions by which resources passed from the colonies to the metropolitan countries were not voluntary nor negotiated by equals. Military force, slave labour and other undue pressures have created moral debts. They claim that investments should, therefore, take account of these bills which are owing.

It is on these moral debts that emphasis is placed by those who complain of the injustice of the present patterns of investment. The moral debts include more than money morally owing. They cover

the harm done to people in the colonial period. The damage done
to the dignity and human nature of the colonial peoples by subjuga-
tion and oppression is assessed very highly by those who are writing
the history of the colonial period in Africa, Asia and Latin America.
Granted that economics is a competitive business, the point they
make is that the ex-colonial people have been maimed before the
competition starts.

This moral argument needs more careful assessment than is normally given to it. But it is doubtful whether the moral recrimination
that goes on will really do any good. What is true is that continual
exploitation harms the economic prospects of the ex-colonial powers
themselves. It is in the interests of the developed nations and of
the corporations which operate from them to improve the economy
of the developing countries. Apart from the fact that exploitation
increases the political risk that these countries may put themselves
under the communist flag of China, it also disables them from
purchasing goods produced in the developed countries. The more
affluent the developing countries become, the greater the markets
which they provide for world trade.

Of the arguments put forward from both sides, it is the last which
is the most realistic. The object of the whole exercise is development, and it is important to remove the explosive elements from
the situation which are introduced by moral arguments. Wholesale
condemnation of past colonial powers is only calculated to entrench
the parties in opposite camps and embitter relationships at a time
when every ounce of goodwill is required in the development effort.
The economic facts are that both the developed and the underdeveloped suffer from failure to produce economic growth in the
poorer countries. The political facts, similarly, are that the widen-
ing gap between rich and poor nations is a danger to peace because
the poor countries are in this way driven to look for other allies.

Passing from the investment debate to the neo-colonial aspects
of the official economic relations between developed and developing
nations themselves, we have to consider the issues of the structures
of aid and the conditions of trade between them. The allegation
is that both aid and trade are so used by the developed nations
that the net beneficiaries are the rich nations themselves rather than
those whom they profess to assist. In fact, not only trade but even
aid is so arranged that it becomes an instrument of improving the
economy of the developed countries and making the aided countries
more dependent on them.

It is claimed that the way in which neo-colonial policies are built
into aid is by making the aid conditional, and it is the conditions,
or quality, which are significant. This is particularly true of bilateral
aid which accounts for between 80% and 90% of official aid,

because the bilateral agreements take care of the donor country which does not happen in the case of multilateral or international aid. The usual conditions include the requirements that the transfer of aid shall be in the form of capital goods from the donor country. These transfers generally represent surplus products rather than sacrificial concern. I. M. D. Little[5] speaks of a printing press in Guinea which operates at 5% of capacity, of the snow-ploughs supplied by Russia to that tropical country, and of the canning factory in the Sudan with nothing to can. Then there is the famous Coperbo factory[6] for producing rubber transferred from Illinois, USA, to Brazil, with disastrous consequences.

It is tempting, indeed, to see neo-colonial interests in these transfers of capital goods. The case is strengthened when what is transferred is not creative and productive so as to remove the dependence of the recipients for replacements or so as to establish competitive industries in their own country. This is the case when they are infra-structures, as they generally are, rather than industrial plants; useful but not industrially competitive. Dependence is increased whenever goods supplied call for spare parts and replacements and for the transfer of skills to operate them. There is also the consideration that the goods transferred represent employment provided for workers in the manufacturing and industrial donor country. Another criticism made is that for the transfer of money to enable establishments to be erected, the donor country requires contracts to be put out for tender at competitive rates. This sounds fair enough, but as expatriate firms are able to outbid local firms, much of the money eventually finds itself back in the country of its origin. Moreover, while employment at the high rates is supplied to the foreigner, the local employee has to take the less well-paid jobs

This catalogue of inbuilt interests in the official transfer of gifts from donor countries appears a little mean and ungrateful. The question is how much truth is there in these allegations and what lessons do they teach. From the point of view of the donor countries we get a different perspective on aid. They maintain that, however conditional, the transfer of goods and money does represent an economic sacrifice. Many of the gifts are productive and creative. The provision of infra-structures relieves the economy of the recipient nation and enables it to invest in other needed items. Moreover, it is unreasonable to expect that no conditions be attached, since the donor has political and economic interests to safeguard.

When it is the volume of aid which is being questioned and, to some extent, its quality, the donor country maintains that it has balance of payment problems to contend with. It cannot afford to give away when the national account is in the red. This has been a greater difficulty than is commonly realized since the internal economy of a country is the primary concern of a government and it is difficult to resist pressures from unions and industrialists at home. However, since 1969, the situation has been considerably eased by the arrangement made by the International Monetary Fund for countries with balance of payments problems to draw on the Fund through the Special Drawing Rights provided under the scheme. It is now possible for the developed countries which, in fact, have the biggest balance of payments problems, to allocate money which they can draw towards the assistance of developing countries. The official report of the Colloquium on Monetary Reform says: [7]

> By assisting developed countries, SDRs will indirectly assist developing countries. The adjustment process will be smoother, world trade will grow more harmoniously, and, in particular, aid and private investment in developing countries will be less affected by balance of payments difficulties. This ought to lead to the rapid elimination of tied aid and other restrictive practices in the transfer of real resources to the developing countries ... the increase of aid is in the first place a problem of transferring real resources, and not a problem of liquidity. Considered as a group, the developed countries can increase aid without affecting their balance of payments situation ... With the allocation of SDRs and the improvement of monetary co-operation, these individual balance of payments problems should diminish. This is, therefore, an appropriate time for a long-term commitment for a substantial increase in the transfer of real resources. The balance of payments constraint can no longer be accepted as justification of the niggardly.

In assessing these positions we are again faced with a practical issue concerning the improvement in the quality of aid rather than with a moral judgment. It is true that moral judgments are not irrelevant, but emotions aroused by these judgments do not help to create answers to economic problems. The question is, in the light of the quality of the aid which the donor countries give and find it difficult to change, whether there is a way by which neo-colonial interests can be removed from these gifts.

It is generally agreed that multilateral or international aid removes these interests. The question seems, therefore, to be, how can international aid, which is only 10% to 20% of the aid now transferred, be increased? The suggestion has been made that there should be a direct link between the allocation of SDRs of the International Monetary Fund and aid through the granting of SDRs

to international aid agencies, such as International Development
Aid. It is true that this would require a lengthy process of re-
negotiation of the articles of agreement of the IMF and that a
proportion of the SDRs would become illiquid. In course of time,
however, the difficulties in the way may be removed.

There are, however, aspects of aid which are separate from these
balance of payments and monetary issues and affect the neo-
colonial argument at a more emotional level. In particular, the
policy adopted by the donor country for the supervision of aid.
I. M. D. Little, in his revealing study of aid to Africa, describes
the problems involved. His references to local reactions to the
meticulous detail applied by AID to the supervision of its aid is
not without its amusement for non-Americans.

The AID suffers from some glaring faults. Indeed, I was, especially in East and Central Africa, much impressed by the resentment caused by the Americans. But I believe that, while this
resentment is real, it is probably rather more strongly felt by
British expatriates than by Africans (after discounting the fact
that expatriates felt less need to be polite about the USA).
Furthermore, much of the resentment is explicable in terms of
the unnecessary delays caused by excessive US red tape; the
rigours of US government policy, involving inevitable friction
and delay; their occasional lack of tact when imposing their own
standards, and the excessive living standards of their over-
numerous staff. Not all the resentment is a necessary consequence
of the neo-colonialism supposed to be involved in a close surveillance of aid.[8]

Much the same would be said in Latin America, only it would be
more caustically impolite. It should be said, however, that sweep-
ing statements about the presence of US aid personnel in developing
countries needs considerable correction in the light of the work of
such organizations as the Peace Corps and a growing sensitivity to
aspirations of these countries which their involvement has developed. Nevertheless, there still remains the widespread impression
in the developing countries that the big powers feel that the poor
countries cannot be trusted to handle their own development. This
is why they feel that neo-colonialism is being expressed in the close
supervision of aid. This is resented for the simple reason that
they are being treated like children. Policies of this kind are self-
defeating since they destroy the sense of responsibility which is
needed in the developing countries to make a success of the projects
which the assistance makes possible. A calculated measure of trust
is absolutely essential to the human development of the people by
whom the new nations will be run. Christian faith has much to say

on this question of trust, and not least the doctrine of justification by faith, as we shall see in the last chapter.

Closely allied to the question of the surveillance of aid, is that of allocation of aid to plans or to projects. All developing countries have development plans which contain a number of projects. These plans, while they are subject to revision in the light of experience, form an integral whole and are invariably based on considerable research and study. For instance, in British Honduras the plan is centred very largely on agricultural development. To serve this a number of projects are required, such as agricultural education, agricultural research, land use, processing plants, storage, shipping facilities, marketing. If only one or two projects are chosen for assistance the plan becomes unworkable and the projects abortive. For example, an elaborate project to develop beef farming is useless if there is no abattoir or transportation, or the suitable stock, or the trained personnel.

The tendency, however, has been for aid to be given to projects rather than to plans. This makes it impossible for the country to get its plan going and puts it at the mercy of the decision of the donor country in relation to each separate project. The guarantee of continuity of financing through the adoption by a donor of a whole plan, subject, of course, to revision, would enable rational growth to be made and confidence to be established in the plan. Neo-colonialism is, therefore, being detected and charged against donor countries which adopt the project rather than the programme or plan policy of aid.

On the other hand, I. M. D. Little, writing, however, after only a few months in Africa, is sceptical about the ability of developing countries to carry through their plan. While he concedes that plan aid is better than project aid in ideal circumstances, he nevertheless advises the latter. Writing with the commercial benefit of the donor country to some extent in mind, he says:

But if such presuppositions (i.e. that the recipient is competent to execute its plan) are unrealistic, as they generally are in Africa, then an intolerable amount of the donor's money will be wasted, at least from the point of view of economic development. The donors should resort to 'project' aid ... It implies that the quantity of aid the country receives is left to emerge mainly from the number and size of good projects that can be agreed: it implies likewise that no promised general level of assistance need be agreed in advance ... it implies that donors must satisfy themselves that the project is appropriate in the general framework of the development of the country; in contrast to this, in the case of plan aid, the donor's general acceptance of the plan implies that anything in it is appropriate.

Because of these issues and problems, therefore, there has been considerable doubt about the effectiveness of aid alone to produce the desired development. We have looked at only a few of its faults. Because of them, led by President Kaunda of Zambia, the development slogan some time ago became 'Not aid but trade'. The rationale of this was that if the poorer countries relied more on the marketing of their products than on subsidies, this would induce greater effort, earn more respect and produce a healthier economy. Hence there arose the demand for new arrangements whereby the developing countries could trade their products more profitably. Negotiations have, therefore, been going on continuously on the terms of trade and the provision of markets in the developed countries for the products of the Third World.

But then, as in the case of foreign investments and aid, the interests of the developed countries were being detected in the terms on which trade was being conducted. Trade itself was discovered or alleged to be a means whereby new forms of colonialism were being practised. In particular, the prices were being set by the importing countries to the disadvantage of the exporting primary producing areas of the Third World. The prices of primary commodities were lowered, and those of manufactured goods from the rich industrial countries were raised. The Haslemere Declaration puts it in this way:

1. Two-thirds of Ghana's exports are cocoa.
   Between 1953 and 1961 cocoa exports increased by 71% in volume, but the revenue only increased by 23%. Meanwhile, manufactured goods shipped to Ghana have gone up to 11% in cost. This means that a machine that cost Ghana the equivalent of 10 tons of cocoa in 1953 cost 15·4 tons of cocoa in 1961. [It is unfortunate that 1953 should be chosen since this was the time of the Korean War when prices of primary products were inflated.]
2. Half of Brazil's exports are coffee.
   Between 1953 and 1961 coffee exports increased by 9% in value but the revenue fell by 35%.
3. Half of Malaya's exports are rubber.
   Between 1960 and 1961 rubber exports increased by 4% in volume but the revenue fell by 35%.
   Desperately trying to maintain their ability to import, the poor countries have borrowed money from the rich, accepted aid, and welcomed private investment. The result, still more economic dependence. They have to borrow more and more in order to repay past loans.

So there has been a concerted demand for price stabilization at an acceptable level. This has been a matter for endless negotiations. But frequently agreement on prices is accompanied by a limitation of import quotas, as in the Commonwealth Sugar Agreements. This brings us to the question of quotas which have been used to limit the trading ability of the poorer countries. Unfortunately, quotas of manufactured goods into industrial countries are forced upon governments in order to protect the interests of the workers and industrialists. This is understandable when the goods come from other industrial countries. But this has a very bad effect on the development of those countries which because of their lower labour costs are sometimes able to produce competitively on the world market, and to discriminate against them is difficult to justify. The Haslemere Declaration again says:

The developing countries have to diversify exports. India and Pakistan, for example, produce low-cost textiles. But when they showed that they were likely to capture most of the British textile market, Britain put quotas on the amount of their textiles that could be imported. The quotas apply only to 'low cost', that is, poor countries, not to the producers in other rich countries.

Other forms of domination that have been identified in the trading relations of rich with poor countries are the use of tariffs on those imported goods which are also produced in the rich countries. The tariffs caused the price of the imported goods to rise, though their cost of production is considerably less than in the importing country. The same effect is produced by the subsidizing by the developed country of products which are traditionally and more economically produced in the developing countries. The subsidizing of sugar-beet in East Anglia and in Holland has caused demonstrations to be made by many concerned about the effect of the subsidized sugar-beet industries on the cane-sugar producing countries of the Caribbean and elsewhere.

The power of the developed nations to dominate the poor countries in trading relations is so strong that they have become almost completely dependent. An instance quoted in the Haslemere Declaration comes from Brazil which was forced to place an export tariff on its coffee sold in the US in order to raise the price so that US soluble coffee would be competitive with it. Non-compliance with the demand would have resulted in a refusal to renew the International Coffee Agreement which maintains stable prices.

We have reached a point where we can now reflect on the aid and trade arrangements and make some kind of assessment. Obviously, the Haslemere Declaration is too highly charged to provide by itself a calm atmosphere for reflection on this very important subject. It has served a useful purpose in alerting public consciences, but it has to be set against other considerations. Moreover, it is not analytical enough in its approach. What considerations should be taken into account?

The following factors seem to be relevant. First of all, there is the given international structure of separate national economic units, each in competition with one another. Decisions concerning aid and trade, therefore, become a matter of bargaining between nations without any arbitration. This places the power in the hands of those with the greatest wealth and means. Secondly, each national unit is responsible ultimately to its own people and is obliged to put its interests first. There are political constraints upon national leaders which compel them to give heed to this principle. Thirdly, within each national unit there are different sectional interests which are affected by aid and trade arrangements. The Workers' Unions are affected by a shift of production from their own country to another. The interests of the industrialists are similarly involved whenever this happens, or when tariff arrangements are changed.

This amounts to saying that the structure of world economics is basically competitive. The principle of altruism is not applicable to it, and it only creates emotional blockages to assume that it is. Until the international economic structures are changed so as to conform more closely to those found in the national structures themselves, where mechanisms of equalization, such as taxation, are used, another principle has to be applied. It is that of human enlightened self-interest. It is in the interests of both developed and developing countries to work towards greater equality both because peace is endangered by economic divisions and because economic prosperity is indivisible. Development is a uniform process which affects the whole human family. This is clear from the fact, so relevant to this discussion, that it is in the interests of the rich countries that the economy of the poorer countries should be improved so that they can purchase their goods. As these goods become more sophisticated and expensive, the wealthier the poor become, the better for trade. The greater the trade the better the communications in a global society.

There is also the more subtle and invisible human consideration. The humanity of the developed peoples of the world is affected by the present world inequalities. Human happiness depends very largely on true community from which sectional pressures are removed, where man can deal openly and honestly with man, where deception and oppression do not warp the personality of those who use them and where inordinate wealth does not taint the heart and soul through the power and fear mechanism which it activates. In the light of what is happening to the developed world as a result of being wealthy in a global village, it is becoming increasingly clear that there is a need to present the meaning of humanity more effectively to it.

There are, of course, two kinds of enlightened self-interest which need to be clearly identified. There is that self-interest which is enlightened by political and economic power considerations. This is frequently the argument put forward to justify concessions in trade and aid arrangements by the donor nations to their own people. In this case it is to increase one's friends in the political power struggle and get more customers for one's goods. The other kind of self-interest is also political and economic. But in this case politics and economics are not interpreted in terms of power. They are understood against the background of the need to develop one political and economic world society in the interests of peace. Truly enlightened self-interest takes account of the need to create political and economic world community. Aid and trade at the higher level of strategy should be commended for this ultimate aim, while it has the immediate effect of making friends and customers.

We have spent some time assessing allegations that neo-colonial interests are built into the economic policies of the developed countries in the fields of investment, aid and trade. We now turn to another instrument of neo-colonialism which is frequently referred to. It is the indirect use of military force to secure the political and economic interests of the developed countries. Military power is not used in the same open way as it was in colonial days when it supported the direct administration of the territory by the colonial power and a full-scale occupation was in operation. Today it is used more subtly and indirectly to support less developed countries to carry on a war by proxy on behalf of the major powers which are really in conflict.

The two instances of this which are usually cited are, first of all, Vietnam, and now Cambodia, where the two major powers of the East and West support opposing political regimes. Russia and China, on the one hand, and the USA and her allies on the other, are engaged in a military struggle where North and South Vietnam stand proxy for them while they supply the weapons and skills of war. The other instance is the Middle East, where Israel and the Arab States stand proxy for the same two major powers. It may be better to limit conflict through proxy arrangements than to allow a nuclear war to develop, but it is the weaker, less developed countries which are the pawns in the game.

Inside the developing countries themselves also, the extension of the power interests of the developed nations through various forms of military involvement is becoming a major concern of the Third World. The presence of military advisers from the powerful nations

and the supply of arms to reactionary and revolutionary governments and groups in the political interests of the West or East is
regarded, quite rightly, as an abuse of power. The weaker countries,
such as Czechoslovakia or Brazil, become tools and instruments
of the political interests of the major powers.

It is not necessarily the political interest which is the main consideration when indirect military power is used in the way described. The Haslemere Declaration quotes the case of Guatemala
where military power was invoked to retain economic interests.

Military involvement by East or West in developing countries
in the political and economic interests of either side scarcely needs
discussion. It is rejected by the enlightened conscience of the modern
world as both unjust and unwise. It is unjust because it is invariably
repressive and maintains inequalities with consequent human
suffering. It is unwise because it creates widespread resentment
against the occupying power and distrust of its general policies. It
also encourages the opposite world power to follow the same
example wherever it may find it convenient and profitable to do so.
The time has come for the question of their military involvement
in developing countries to be made a major issue of discussion
between the major powers with a view to their complete withdrawal
and settlement of terms on which they would agree to refrain from
military interference. It is naïve to expect one power to make a
unilateral decision to withdraw. In that case an attempt should
be made to reach a general agreement.

The third area where neo-colonialism is being detected by those
within the developing countries who are concerned about the new
forms of dependence and domination which are arising as a result
of the involvement of the richer countries in the development of the
poorer ones, is that of culture. It is difficult to determine where
economics end and culture begins, but the argument is, nevertheless, quite clear and simple. We will take the example of technology to illustrate the argument.

Before we do so, let us be clear what we mean by culture, a
subject which we shall discuss in the next chapter at greater length.
By a culture we mean the way of life of a people, the commonly
accepted aims and assumptions on which habits, ways of thought
and expression are based, including values and beliefs. A culture
usually has a geographical spread. It tends to get modified in those
areas where it comes into contact with other cultures. This contact
has social and other effects. Generally speaking, religious belief has
a formative effect on a culture, but it is also possible and, perhaps,
probable that a culture can be traced back to the economic basis of
the life of the people. We observe this, for instance, in isolated
Kekchi Maya communities in British Honduras. Their family struc-

ture, their mores, their total life is based on the need to live off the milpa, or movable piece of ground cut out of the forest. The family unit is structured by this need, and duties and obligations are determined by it. Their religious belief before they became Christians was also conditioned by their economic needs. In other words, economics and culture go very closely together.

When, therefore, S. C. Parmar, the noted ecumenical Indian economist,[9] says that the export of technology from the West to the developing countries is a means of domination, he means that both economic and cultural forces are set in motion to create new patterns of dependence in the developing countries. He says:

> Technology is power, and that power is never neutral. It becomes the carrier of those systems and ideologies within which it has been nurtured. For the poorer nations, too much of the present transfer of technology is a projection of the economic needs of the givers rather than a response to the needs of the receivers.

In the next chapter we shall deal with the question of culture and development and discuss the debate going on between those, on the one hand, who hold that the culture of the East must yield to the technological demands of development and accept the consequent changes, and those, on the other hand, who hold a different view about cultural transformation. Here we are concerned with the more limited question of the neo-colonial interests which are built into the transfer of technology from West to East. What is alleged is that these interests are built into this transfer by means of extending the dependence of the recipient on the donor in two ways.

In the first place, the production and use of technology is related to the cultural aims and assumptions of the West. This, of course, refers particularly to scientific technology which is those means made possible by scientific research. This process of producing scientific technology is backed by an intricate cultural background in the West, built around not only the Christian doctrine of creation which could be disputed, but also, and more particularly, the Graeco-Roman culture. It is spelled out in education and education methods, language, terms, books, and personnel, and in aims which are not part of the parcel of eastern culture. To produce technology and even to use it, creates a cultural dependence on its cultural home in the West. The users of technology have to pass through an education process which is organized in the West, and they have to adopt the same aims and assumptions. By changing aims and assumptions what is meant is that eastern cultures have to change their whole attitude to the purposes of life and alter their systems of values in order to embrace technology fully. It means accepting the gadget and wealth culture of the West in place of the less material values of their present or past cultures.

The second way in which scientific technology creates dependence on the West is equally subtle. Scientific technology is an integral whole. Not only is it based on a highly organized and widely spread scientific research and teaching programme through universities, schools and institutes which complement one another. The production and maintenance of these scientifically-based techniques are also part of an intricate technological industrial system where specialization and precision are woven into an integral and co-ordinated scheme financed in an equally intricate way. It is only within this complicated system that the technological instruments can be created, and it is only from this base that they can be supplied and maintained.

There are a number of considerations which arise out of this issue to which attention should be paid when assessing dependence and domination factors which are operative in technological industrial relations between developed and developing countries. To begin with, there are degrees of dependence which vary from one article to the next. For instance, the degree of dependence within the Coca-Cola empire is not as great as that within the General Motor empire because people can do without Coca-Cola, but trucks and transport vehicles have to be maintained and replaced. The degree of dependence varies, therefore, according to the availability of alternatives and the dispensability of the techniques. This means, of course, that the purchaser in the developing country must exercise discernment about the necessity of the articles offered for sale or as a gift. Apart from the few exceptions the great industrial empires are not built without the consent of the purchasers.

Allied to this is another consideration – that development in its initial stages is more closely linked with thrift than with consumption. It is those countries which have abstained from consuming imports and exercised restraint in the use of foreign-produced techniques which have had the healthiest form of development. What it means is that a good deal more consultation, negotiation and planning needs to be done concerning the transfer of techniques from a rich to a poor society, and a much higher representation from the developing countries should be included in these consultations from the start. Through open discussion and carefully prepared planning one side can come to understand the other and the exploitation and harmful reactions can be lessened.

The fourth area where neo-colonialism has often been detected is in overseas service of personnel from the developed countries. This is of two kinds. There is that given through technical assistance programmes when experts are transferred for temporary service in a developing country either for advisory purposes or for more direct involvement. These are usually supplied through aid programmes. There is also what is given in the form of shorter term voluntary service, generally through government, sometimes through other organizations, such as Peace Corps, Canadian University Service Overseas, British Voluntary Service Overseas and CIIR, Papal Volunteers and, more recently, German organizations.

Assessments made of these services vary considerably. Much depends on the personality of the expert or volunteer. There are a number of casualties, and there are very many real successes. The technical value of their services in societies with very limited expertise but with ambitious development plans cannot be overestimated. Education programmes, particularly in secondary schools, technical and teachers' colleges and universities, in many countries, would be severely curtailed without their help. The advisory services provided by voluntary agencies for many government administrative sectors have often been indispensable. Many places would be without adequate, often without any, medical services but for those provided by volunteers and personnel supplied under technical aid schemes.

To allege neo-colonialism in this situation seems to require a great deal of credibility. Nevertheless, just as the missionary activity of the church in the colonial period is sometimes accused of being the moral arm of imperialism, though without conscious complicity in the imperial exercise, so the overseas technical and voluntary service programmes of developed countries are accused of being the agents of neo-colonialism, albeit well-intentioned. However, the criticism is tempered both by appreciation of these motives and the volunteers and experts themselves personally and by the consciousness of the need for them. Frank criticism made with the intention of removing the abuses, however, should be heard.

The usual criticisms are that the expert and the volunteer bring with them assumptions and ideas which belong to their own culture. This is inevitable but the effects can be unfortunate, especially where the expatriate is insensitive to the cultural values and the social and economic structure of the country where he is serving. Deriving his way of living and doing things from what is done 'back home' – a most dangerous expression to use in a developing country – if he is not sensitive to the situation he finds himself trying to make contact with the people within the terms of his own culture. The culture gap, however, is usually too wide between him and the ordinary people and he normally tends to find refuge in a like-minded circle within that society. When this happens the object of the presence of the volunteer in developing countries is defeated, since his service can only be effective if he succeeds in some measure in identifying himself with the people themselves. This requires of the volunteer a sensitivity and a sympathy which, unfortunately, is not always found. Ivan Illich had some rather caustic remarks to make about the type of volunteer who fails to identify and does not realize his inability to do so. Speaking to a group of American students doing voluntary service in Mexico he said:

> Not only is there a gulf between what you have and what others have which is much greater than the one existing between you and the poor in your country, but there is also a gulf between what you feel and what the Mexican people feel that is incomparably greater ... The only people with whom you can hope to communicate are some members of the middle class. And here please remember that I said 'some' – by which I mean a tiny *élite* in Latin America ... Some years ago your country began and financed a so-called 'Alliance for Progress'. This was an 'Alliance' for the progress of the middle class *élites*. Now, it is among the members of this middle class that you will find a few people who are willing to waste their time with you. And they are overwhelmingly those 'nice kids' who would also like to soothe their troubled conscience by doing something nice for the promotion of the poor Indians.

Of course, Illich is stretching it a little and his language does not show that sympathetic appreciation which the volunteer often deserves. While one must admit the truth of much that he says about an inbuilt paternalism in the motivation of the volunteer from a rich society serving in a poor country, we must also recognize that many of these volunteers have shown a sensitivity to local situations and people which is commendable. If a volunteer tends to assume authority in certain situations, this is a regrettable revelation of the actual relationship of rich and poor nations, but it is, nevertheless, unfortunate, and I would say, ungrateful, not to recognize the high motivation of the volunteer even if he often fails to express it in an ideal way. The cool of Illich's beautiful Cuernavaca does not encourage one to appreciate the devotion and dedication of those who serve in the sticky heat and socially deprived places in tropical under-developed areas of the world.

The volunteer must discover the most appropriate form which his presence should take in developing countries. Generally this means that he has to refrain from obtruding himself or giving any appearance of assuming leadership. Wherever he fails in this respect, his service is resented and whatever the appearances to the contrary, he does not really succeed.

What, however, is not so easily realized is that the initiative which the volunteer or the expatriate from the advanced society demonstrates is only a reflection of the initiative which that society takes in the total development plan and programme. It is significant, though seldom noticed, that it is in the West that much of the concern is expressed, the advice is given, the plans made and the initiative taken for the development of the less privileged areas of the world. Much of the planning is done from the point of view of the developed world. The initiative is taken there. The standards are set there. The developing Third World finds that the decisions have already been taken and the positions already adopted by the more powerful who are 'concerned' about their development and have made their plans to help them. Herein lies one of the basic faults of the whole development enterprise. The initiative is taken not by those who have to implement the plans and live with the future, but by those who can withdraw into their own castles if they fail.

These considerations have led to new thinking about voluntary service. The following suggestions have been put forward[10] in *Risk* under the significant title of 'Good Will and Evil Goods'. First and foremost there should be a redefinition of voluntary service; this redefinition, however, must be done not by the voluntary service organization itself. It must be done by the countries where the voluntary service is actually exercised. They must say what they want done. Secondly, there must be greater participation by the developing countries in voluntary service programmes, in particular by sharing in this service within other developing countries where there is a closer affinity between them and these countries than between them and the developed countries. In this way, they can strengthen one another more effectively by a common background than can be done by the voluntary service of those who do not enter into their experience at the depth of real identification. Thirdly, volunteers need to know much more about the political and economic factors which affect the underdeveloped countries so that their service can be made more relevant. The question remaining is: Will the developed countries be willing to spend the same amount of money on the promotion of voluntary service undertaken by people in the developing countries as they do on their own volunteers?

NOTES

1. *Responsible Government in a Revolutionary Age*, article by John Karefa Smart, 'African Nationalism – the Aftermath of Colonialism'.
2. Review Article by John Barnabas on *Uppsala Report, World Development* (Beirut Report) and *Line and Plummet* in *International Review of Mission*, Vol. LVIII, No. 232, Oct. 1969, p. 465.
3. Art. cit., p. 279.

4. See above, ch. 2.
5. *Aid to Africa*, p. 21.
6. See *Development Apocalypse*, Risk Paperback, Issues 1 and 2, WCC 1967, p. 22.
7. *Money in a Village World*, pp. 20, 21.
8. See *Aid to Africa*, pp. 35ff.
9. See reference to 'Exploratory Conference on Technology and the Future of Man and Society', held in July 1970 in Geneva, sponsored by WCC, in EPS, 3 July 1970, p. 4, and *This Month*, EPS, July 1970, p. 7. Report not yet available.
10. See *Risk*, Vol. 6, No. 2, 1970, p. 12.

6

The Divided Soul - Culture and Modernization

In the black society of the USA a black man who follows the habits of white culture or is known to be out of step with the Black Power movement is sometimes called an 'oreo-cookie'.[1] This is a thick, double chocolate wafer with white cream filling inside. This is a good way to introduce the kind of situation in which non-western people find themselves when they meet the culture of the West. They have to live at two levels. At one level they take on western customs; at the other, they continue their own. The Japanese, who have created the most modernized society in the East, symbolized this very well when they lived in a house of two storeys between which there was no stairway. The upper storey was furnished in western style and the lower in Japanese. You will find it also in the Caribbean where an educated black man will speak in a perfect Oxford accent and yet retain the ability to speak in Creole. Something similar, of course, occurs in English class society when a man leaves the lower class in which he was born and moves up into another with its own cultural nuances.

This is the condition of what one might call a divided soul, where one half of a man is attuned to the thoughts and ways of his original culture and the other half aspires to the benefits which belong to a different way of life. But it is far more acute in some parts of the world than in others. In the English setting it is the accepted thing to move from one class to the other and adopt all the signs which accompany the cultural movement upwards, of 'Keeping up with the Joneses', moving from football pools to bridge parties, from one make of car to another, from the local school to the preparatory school, and so on. This is a shared ambition of most English people. Even political socialism has to emphasize a policy of levelling in an upward direction rather than the kind of equalization which brings down the standards for those who are already at a higher level. It has to exalt the humble and meek without bringing down the mighty from their seat, or sending the rich empty away.

In England the divided soul, which is symbolized by the class society itself and expressed in the subdued resentments between them, is knit together again by a more inclusive culture which binds together the sub-cultures of the classes. This common culture subdues the tensions between them. One of the assumptions which binds them together is the common aim of modernization, or progress in social and economic development through scientific technology, in spite of all the trouble it causes!

In many non-western societies it is quite different. Modernization, as it has come to them, contradicts the basic assumptions and aims and, consequently, the way of life of many of these societies. The division in the soul of the Asian who aspires to the benefits of a modern society but whose culture will not allow of the assumptions and, therefore, of the disciplines which make western modernization possible, is very deep indeed. For he wants, but he cannot avail himself, of these benefits without adopting a new culture.

One can better understand the cleavage in the heart of peoples moving from their old condition to one of modernity when it is compared with the movement of people from poverty to greater affluence in developed societies. Poverty has a culture of its own where the quality of life, particularly in human relationships, is different from affluence. In poverty people have a greater sense of community, a greater willingness to share, and a strange familiarity with suffering which gives them a sense of security and, because it is there already, takes away fear of deprivation. When they move into better social conditions, usually through some new housing project, their problems change because their relationships and their situation change. They move into a new culture where economic values predominate. In gaining greater economic and social advantages they lose also some of those things which in the sub-culture of poverty had given their life a human quality of which the wealth, so important to their physical well-being, had deprived them. They become unhappy when they gain what they want because their soul has to be adjusted to wealth. They are disillusioned. This is something like the division which modernization causes in the soul of developing peoples in whose previous culture wealth has not played a dominant role.

There are two causes of this cleavage in the soul of many non-western societies which is induced by contact with the wealthy West. The first is religion. Many of these societies have cultures which are based on a religion or a religious outlook which has a different attitude to nature from that which has been inherited in the West with its origins in Graeco-Roman-Hebrew culture.[2] In non-western societies generally, nature is in different degrees and forms regarded as sacral, or else it is regarded as so intimately bound up with human life, as in Africa, that the manipulation of nature is believed to have repercussions on man's welfare. On the other hand, Christianity has given the West freedom to subdue the creation, Greek civilization has given it its science by which it can study nature, and Roman culture has encouraged it to use this science to dominate and impose human will upon it through technology. Generally speaking, therefore, wherever Hinduism, Buddhism or primitive animism has been the predominant religion, contract with the West has led to cultural cleavage where one half of the soul wants modernization and the other refuses to abandon its religious assumptions and beliefs.

The second cause of cleavage is partly political. Modernization started in the West. It appeared in the Third World during the colonial period when it was handled and managed by the imperial power. It was a completely western imperialist phenomenon. During the post-colonial independence era, the politicians have tried to get rid of every trace of the old imperialism. Nevertheless, they want the benefits of modernization. Hence the cleavage in the soul.

However, the resistance to modernization, backed as it is by the resurgence of the old religions in Asia, is not without justification wherever it is simply the manifestation of a western process. For unless it is supported by the culture of the country, it remains an artificial importation and has unfortunate social and cultural consequences. Nor can the development process be sustained unless it is rooted in the national culture. For it is only a development process, which does not destroy the cultural identity of a people and thus does not take their dignity away from them, which will not in the end prove to be a delusive mirage and produce reactions against development itself. People have to be engaged at that level in their life which motivates them. This means the level at which they not only give intellectual assent but are also emotionally sustained.

This leads us straight into the problem of modernization in the Third World. There seem to be three questions. The first is whether modernization is possible without accepting western culture? Is modernization equivalent to westernization?

First of all, let us see what modernization means. John Hall of the University of Michigan, who has done considerable study of Japanese cultural change in the process of modernization, has given the following criteria[3]: (1) a comparatively high degee of urbanization; (2) widespread literacy; (3) comparatively high *per capita* income; (4) extensive geographical and social mobility; (5) relatively high degree of commercialization and industrialization within the economy; (6) an extensive and penetrating network of mass communications media; (7) widespread participation and involvement of members of the society in modern, social and economic processes; (8) a relatively highly-organized bureaucratic form of government with widespread involvement of members of the society; (9) an increasingly rational and secular orientation of the individual to his environment based on the growth of scientific knowledge. There are, of course, variables which modify and change these criteria by which we identify modernization.

Accepting these as criteria, we are faced with our question whether modernization requires the adoption of western culture for its promotion. Japan, which is the most advanced modern state in the non-western world, has provided the most relevant material for the study of this question. An important case study was made on this question a few years ago by a team of American scholars. Their conclusions were that the modernization of Japan in terms of the criteria which we have listed was largely due to modern Japanese nationalism under the emperor system. This means that the change from one way of life to another through technological and industrial revolution was motivated from within by awakened national consciousness through which Japan passed during this period. It was not an external imposition or adoption, but arose from within the potential of Japanese culture itself realized by political ambition.

A similar conclusion is reached by John F. Fairbanks, Edwin O. Reischauer and Albert M. Craig.[4] They deal with the same question of modernization and westernization under the heading of the controversy over adoption versus adaption. They show by extensive evidence that modernization in Japan as well as in China and other countries in the East, is taking place within the traditional context. They say 'There is no reason to suppose that a thoroughly modernized East Asia will be merely a reflection of the modernized West either in its superficial cultural patterns or in its fundamental ideals and values.'[5] This conclusion is heavily supported by the evidence of the cultural revolution under Mao Tse-Tung, which is largely motivated by the policy to remove all traces of western culture left after the colonial period, and to enable the economic revolution to be carried entirely by forces within Chinese culture itself as it is transformed to meet the challenge of a new society. Modernization does, therefore, appear to be possible without taking over western culture.

These conclusions, however, have been based on the assumption that the support given to modernization from within eastern culture has been due to motivation supplied by technological and economic factors; that it is because of the attractions of a technological economy that these people have moved so easily into modernization. Many Japanese scholars and, among them even Marxist intellectuals, have questioned this kind of evaluation of Japanese society and culture. They stress that it is not only economic prosperity which gives meaning and direction to the dynamically changing Japanese society. There are other inner motives, value concepts and a kind of ethos which direct and form the change. There is, therefore, an emphasis among Japanese scholars on the importance of the value concepts within their own culture as factors basic to the modernization of Japan which is not to be understood merely in technological and economic terms.

In particular, considerable attention has been paid to the potential which the concept of man in Japanese culture possesses, as an internal driving force for the modernization of society. Mention is frequently made of the work of three Japanese scholars.[6] One is Hisao Otsaka, a leading Christian economist of Tokyo University. Working along the lines of Max Weber's *Protestant Ethic and the Spirit of Capitalism*, his emphasis is upon the ethics of man which makes possible the structural reformation of society. This ethic, derived from Protestantism, finds a response in the Japanese who by means of it transform their society. His concern is to repudiate the Marxist theory of a deterministic economic development, and to show that modernization is not the result of such a mechanical process but of human response ethically conditioned. Another is Masao Marugama, who has made a close study of the basis and logic of Japanese thought. He has discovered through his studies of the thought of intellectual leaders in Japan that within the culture itself the potential existed in its concept of man to carry forward the modernizing process. The other is Yoshimi Takenshi who offers a challenge to Asian man to rise out of his stagnation. He resists the cultural impact of the West and calls for the growth of indigenous selfhood similar to the challenge of Lu Hsun who has had such an influence on the humanist movement in the East. His cry is 'From below and into within, but never from outside and unto upward'. These three thinkers appeal to something basic already in Japanese culture as the lever for development. It is the concept of man.

Political leaders, also, have been concerned during the independence era to find a basis in their own culture for the changes which political independence requires and for the new economic efforts called for. They had to dig deep into their past and into the foundations of their culture. Some, however, have complained that Africa's past has been so cut off by the colonial period which had made the people ashamed of their own culture, that it has been emotionally impossible to recover it.

Nkrumah,[7] however, does find in African culture a basis on which to build a new human society because of the place which man has in that culture. It is also the basis of his particular African kind of socialism. He says:

> The traditional face of Africa includes an attitude towards man which can only be described, in its social manifestation, as being socialist. This arises from the fact that man is regarded in Africa as primarily a spiritual being, a being endowed originally with a certain inward dignity, integrity and value ... Herein lies the theoretical basis of African communalism. This theoretical basis expressed itself on the social level in terms of institutions, such as the clan, underlining the equality of all, and the responsibility of many for one. In this social situation, it was impossible for classes of a Marxian kind to arise. By a Marxian kind of class, I mean one which has a place in a horizontal social stratification.

In India, Gandhi who was in many ways a traditionalist and wedded to Hinduism was, nevertheless, persuaded that the future of his country was bound up with its political development in a democratic direction. He was a keen advocate of the equality of people and opposed the caste system and downgrading of women. For his policy he searched in Indian history and culture, and he was followed by several other Indian statesmen.

> India has been a democracy in the modern sense of the term only during the last ten years. From this point of view we are an infant democracy. But we cannot forget that democratic traditions in India have been in existence from time immemorial. A study of Indian history shows that the village Republics continued to function in India even after the advent of British rule. From this point of view, therefore, India must be considered a mature and ancient democracy.[8]

On the other hand, there have been those who have been convinced that the only successful cultural base for modernization is provided through the adoption of westernization. One of these is Van Leeuwen, who in his remarkable book *Christianity in World History*, has described how the impact of western technological culture has changed the cultural ethos of eastern societies and made modernization possible. This has been through a contradiction of the basic religious assumptions of the East which western culture, founded as it is on Christianity and Graeco-Roman culture, has brought through the advance of technology from the West. This is a conclusion which Arnold Toynbee[9] has also reached as a result of his historical studies in this area. It has been remarked that Van Leeuwen has invested western technological culture with messianic dimensions, and handed over the mission of conversion from the church to western technological and economic forces which are changing the culture of the East. With the support of such impressive evidence based on historical research as is provided by Van Leeuwen and Toynbee, it is not strange that the general assumption of most people in the West is that the East should swallow the whole culture package delivered by it and become completely westernized.

It is from within the Third World that the strongest reactions are registered against this assumption and the westernization which gives it credence. It is possible to identify three forms of reaction. The first is the powerful resurgence of indigenous religions within the cultures most affected by the challenge of westernization. The resurgence of Buddhism, Islam and Hinduism, as well as other religions, is largely due to reactions against the West. At the end of the nineteenth century it produced the militant nationalism of Tilak which was carried on into the early part of this century. In Africa it produced the Mau Mau movement with its violent anti-white atrocities in the early 1950s. Similar reactions without the violence have been evidenced in Ceylon where the Buddhist and Sinhala faiths asserted their traditionalism soon after independence. In the Caribbean, the most westernized of all societies, the period following independence is now witnessing a search for a cultural base other than that inherited from the West during the colonial period, to carry on the development process. The struggle for a viable independence is also closely linked with the search for a Caribbean cultural identity which is based on the experience and background of the people. The reaction against westernization is probably also the cause of the acceptance of Mohammedanism by some of the leaders of the Black Power movement which identifies whiteness with western as against African culture. This is why Arthur Mayhew, the British educationist, claims that it is a mistake to impose western culture on other societies, and calls for a change from within their cultures rather than for their negation.

The second reaction to westernization has been the search by scholars and religious leaders for a base within these cultures upon which modernization can be securely founded. Mention has already been made of the studies conducted of Japanese culture. These, however, are only an instance of a general intellectual concern throughout non-western academic circles to find indigenous sources in their human culture for the development which they desire. One of these concerns is centred upon the potential of Hindu culture to assimilate and even to produce technology. Christians have prided

themselves on the assumption that science and technology have
arisen within the culture where Christianity has been the dominant
religion. They have traced the cause of this to the biblical understanding of creation and of man's responsibility. Some Hindu
scholars, however, anxious to find a base for technological development in Hindu culture, dispute the exclusive claims of Christianity
to the conception and birth of science and technology. They trace
a line of continuity from their modern manifestation and acceptance
in Hindu culture back to some of its basic concepts which can be
illustrated from history.

Christians in India also have looked for avenues within Hinduism
for modernization. It has been one of the great contributions of
the Christian Institute for the Study of Religion and Society at
Bangalore, to have assisted the passage of India from a Hindu
sacral culture to a secular pluralism through the studies of Hinduism
itself which have been conducted at the Institute.

Another instance of a search within the indigenous culture for
a base for modernization is the modern cultural revolution in
China. This movement originated from a reaction against western
imperialism which drove Mao Tse-Tung to look for concepts and
assumptions in Chinese culture which would displace those provided
by the West. The resulting economic transformation is widely
believed to be due at least in part to the enlisting of forces in
China's culture in the service of modernization.

The third reaction to westernization has already been mentioned.
It is the reaction caused by the sociological effects of the introduction of western culture into other societies. The two-tier culture
mentioned at the beginning of this chapter which has been inherited
by countries from their political dependence on the western powers
during the colonial period, and their continued economic and
technological domination by them, is having human and economic
effects to which sociologists and social anthropologists have been
drawing attention in recent years. The fact that the two-tier culture
tends to follow the 'haves' and 'have-nots' economic tiers has
strengthened the case of the sociologists who are pointing to the
dangers of the westernization of indigenous cultures. They say it is
producing this gap because the 'haves' are westernized groups who
have economic ties with the West and speak its 'language'.

Nevertheless, of course, there is general acknowledgment that
whereas westernization is not essential to modernization, the impact of the West upon other cultures has been responsible for the
rise of modernization in societies where the culture has been
traditionalist and stagnant. M. M. Thomas[10] sums it up by saying:

I would grant that western culture can stimulate the creative process of indigenization of the spirit of modernity, and also that technology carries with it the idea of secular rationality and the cultural ferment to which the gospel of Christ gave birth. But those who hope that the growth of industrialization and urbanization, with their accompanying secularization, will in the near future create a new ethos which will displace the religious and metaphysical *weltanschauung* of traditional societies, are likely to be disappointed. Radical westernization of culture may be possible for isolated individuals living in a non-western culture or for some very backward cultures, but it is not practical for a whole advanced culture.

The next question which the problems of modernization and culture present is whether modernization can be sustained in the Third World without a transformation of the cultures within it. Transformation, of course, here means change of the culture without adopting another foreign culture. Up to this point we have regarded modernization as the absorption by a society of the material and social technology necessary to increase productivity and standards of living. The criteria which we considered earlier in this chapter, proposed by John Hall, are centred upon the economic process and the social consequences resulting from it. This was put forward as the meaning of modernization.

The question with which we are now faced is whether this is enough. Is there not a need also for cultural change or transformation to make this modernization possible? Or, indeed, is the economic interpretation of modernization or development sufficient in itself? Many, particularly in the developing countries, dispute this and regard the limited economic and technological interpretation as typical of the attitude of the developed nations towards the culture of these societies. Modernization, they claim, is more than the provision of material and social technology. It includes the culture of the people and those things which belong to the specifically human. There is need, they say, not only for economic and social change but also for cultural transformation whereby the people themselves and their culture are transformed within the total process.

What is meant by transformation here, of course, is not a radical break with their cultural past. This break is what happens when they adopt western culture and abandon their own. Transformation means a change from within. There is a continuity with the past which gives personal security and human dignity of which people are deprived when their past culture is denied and negated. In the transformation, what was treasured or assumed in the past culture is developed or transformed as a result of contact with a catalytic

agent from another culture. But it is continuous with the culture
from which it develops. This, I believe, is very important. The
philistinism with which the more technologically advanced societies
treat local and sub-cultures of other societies does immense harm at
the human level and puts local co-operation with the transformation
or modernization of their own societies out of action. Cultural
domination can have as bad effects in the human field as economic
domination is acknowledged to have.

There is, of course, another view on this question which denies
the need for transformation. It deserves attention because it is put
forward by a philosopher of technology who has done considerable
work in this field. It is the view of Robert Theobald which he puts
forward in *New Possibilities in Modern Technology*. He claims that
cybernetics has introduced a new factor into development which
insulates the cultures of people from the effects of modernization.
In the past production was done by human hands and involved
human lives. It therefore had an effect upon their culture and way
of life. Cybernetics transfers the means of production to non-human
instruments. It is, therefore, feasible to conceive of a modernizing
industrial process going on without much effect on the local culture
– a modern economy and an ancient culture living alongside one
another. There are many who agree with Theobald on the grounds
that this is a way by which the values of ancient cultures can be
preserved. They cite the losses, in what they regard as human terms,
which the development process has caused. The gentle people of
the East, with their mystic passivity, who are changed into active,
vigorous, secular persons, is what is in mind. The loss of religious
and ethical concepts in the process, of course, tends to strengthen
their case for insulating ancient cultures from change, made possible
to some extent by cybernation.

The difficulty which Theobald's view creates is threefold. It
exaggerates the applicability of cybernation; it does not take sufficient account of the social effects of cybernetics, and it introduces a
new means of domination by the developed countries over those
which are developing. To explain – while it is true that cybernation
does take over a large area of the production and management
process, and thus creates more leisure, it can never completely take
work out of human hands and it tends to create alternative and new
types of work. Cybernetics itself tends to bring a new type of
society into being, to which older cultures have to be adapted. The
leisure made possible by cybernation has to be used creatively,
which means using it in relation to the society which exists. Culture,
by definition, means cultivation of human life within the social
milieu. It is not an élitism which separates from life. Most damaging
of all, however, is the domination over developing countries by the

sources where cybernation is produced, namely, the West. It would mean keeping the people of the Third World in the bondage of technological ignorance and incompetence, enjoying a mystic religious vision, while the West develops their resources for them through these automatic machines. These will have been produced in the developed countries through research and work provided there.

It is, therefore, not possible to have both the benefit of technologically guided economic development and at the same time retain ancient cultures in the same form in which they existed in the pre-scientific period without considerable unfortunate human consequences. The transformation of culture in the Third World is a necessary consequence of the adoption of modernization, if the other cultural alternative of westernization is not acceptable, as we have already suggested.

What, therefore, do we mean by transformation in this context? Authentic cultural transformation means the changes which occur in the way of life of a people as a result of the activation of forces dormant but already present within the culture itself. The normal cause of cultural change is a new awareness acquired by the people themselves as a result of a change in the social and economic context of their lives. They begin to see themselves differently and, as a result, organize themselves and their way of life differently. Cultural transformation takes place as a result of developments within the specifically human consciousness of people themselves. Changes in the way of life of a people then take place as a result not of innovations and customs imported or imposed upon them from outside, but of changes in the realm of their own consciousness about themselves which produces new attitudes and modifications in ways of living.

The cultural transformation, which happens in response to modernization and facilitates it, is one that occurs as a result of this change in people's consciousness about themselves. People living within what have been called 'fused' cultures where they are lost within an unchanging community where all is predetermined by custom and organized under a ritual cycle which allows no innovations, suddenly become conscious of themselves as persons and individuals when the ritual pattern is broken by economic development. A discovery of the personal and of the human occurs when people begin to be thrown on to their own resources as a result of the 'fused' community giving way to the 'refracted' society. This is when the split into individual, personal units takes place. Individual, personal identity takes the place of a primal, undifferentiated unity which characterizes most ancient cultures. This is when the awakening of peoples begins. It begins with a consciousness of the human element, the discovery of the personal and the claim to be free.

Transformation is then initiated from the point where people discover their human and personal stature. This is the reason why in developing countries the emphasis is upon humanism as the basis from which transformation of their culture must take place. But this humanism must be understood not in terms of the humanistic controversies of the West, but of the change from a communal, fused culture to one based on the personal awakening of people to their human dignity as individual persons. It is human dignity which is the focal point for the transformation of culture and not economic development. This is an emphasis which modern Westerners with their excessive emphasis on material values fail to appreciate. They cannot understand why ways of life should not be changed to accommodate economic advantage, and why some developing countries are so reluctant to accept changes which cause social dislocation and other human mal-effects. It explains, however, the emphasis on humanism in such places as Zambia[11] and India.

What humanism is designed to serve in developing countries is the moral criterion on which a new society is to be formed as a result of community disintegration. Modern technological economic development causes a process of social atomization to occur. The fused community is broken up into individual persons. This leads to the need to reintegrate the individuals into new formations on which they will carry over into their new organization those basic elements in the culture which are essential to their significance as persons.

C. E. Black, in his book *The Dynamics of Modernization*, explains how the process takes place. Using the comparative method he has examined the modernization process in most, if not all, the countries of the world. He divides these countries into seven categories according to certain common historical criteria and finds a general pattern to which they comply in the process of modernization. This general pattern consists of four chronological phases.

First comes the challenge of modernity which is the initial confrontation of a society, within its traditional framework of knowledge, with modern ideas and institutions. This leads to the second phase after the emergence of the advocates of modernity, which is the consolidation of modernizing leadership, sometimes after bitter revolutionary struggles lasting several years. The third phase is that of economic and social change to a point where a society is transformed from a rural and agrarian situation to one that is urban and industrial. The fourth phase is the integration of society where the economic and social transformation produces a fundamental reorganization of the social structure throughout the society.

During the phase of economic and social transformation people

get detached from their traditional settings. Within these settings
they are primarily members of a natural community with its own
culture. They do not stand over against that community as individuals but find their essential functions and being as part of a larger
whole to which they are tied by cultural links. The advent of
economic change sets an atomizing process in motion and the
members of the old traditional community become individuals. They
become aware of themselves as persons. This creates the need for
a new phase of social re-integration of the individual persons. The
atoms have to be gathered into new units. But at this stage they
have become aware of their individuality, which creates problems.

> The concept of integration as used in this connection means in
> particular that the individual's ties with local, regional, and other
> intermediate structures are reduced at the same time that his ties
> with the larger and more diffuse urban and industrial network
> are strengthened. This shift of relationships gives the individual
> the advantages of greater opportunities in a more flexible society
> and a larger share in the distribution of resources in terms of
> education, consumer goods, and a variety of services. It deprives
> him, however, not only of the support and consolation offered by
> membership in a more autonomous community, but also of the
> relative stability of employment and social relations that agrarian
> life provides in normal times.[12]

After this explanation of the process by Black, let us now proceed
to try to understand how cultural transformation is called for in
the various types of culture where modernization has begun to
create the atomization of fused societies. We can identify two types
of culture where this transformation is demanded and has to be
promoted in the interests of a modernization which is truly human.

The first type of culture or aspect which belongs to non-western
culture is that which is described by John Taylor in his important
book, *The Primal Vision*. It describes the nature of African religion
as a vision of 'a total unbroken unity'. In African religion a
continuity runs through the whole of life, including nature, man
and the spirit world, both past and present, binding them up in a
single unity. In this unity man is not an individual separate from
the rest, but the point at which the whole comes to consciousness.
His total being, his health and prosperity, depends upon preserving
a correct relation with the whole *continuum* of nature and the spirit
world. What happens, however, with the impact of modernity
through economic change is that a new sense of individuality occurs
as men break loose from their communal ties. This makes possible
a heightened sense of responsibility and human dignity where men
stand on their own feet over against nature. It is important that the

transformation of culture which is made possible and demanded by development should take account of those things within the culture itself, so that they are used to support people and assist them to express their human nature. In other words, transformation of culture must be done in the interests of humanization. The West must learn to respect this basic human need which leaders in developing countries are already recognizing.

The type of outlook characteristic of African culture, which has been described as an undifferentiated cosmic monism, is not confined to Africa. It has been discovered to be basic to most eastern religions also. It characterizes the culture of China, Japan and India, as well as other countries of the East. In all of these countries a new attitude is emerging as a result of economic change and in place of the primal vision of unity. Differentiation is being manifested and the peculiar nature of man as a responsible person distinct from nature is forming the basis of a new humanism. Special attention is being given to human rights and justice. This is being given a new foundation in the awakened sense of human dignity previously concealed in the undifferentiated whole.

Dr Erna Hoch,[13] a distinguished psychiatrist, who has made a profound study of Indian family structure and its relation to mental health, has drawn attention to the difference between the basis of the family in India and in the West. In India the family is 'the primary root organization of humanity'. All the members are bound together by this primary group into which they are born. This type of person, bound by this relationship, does not possess the qualities of robust individuality and personal responsibility until he is awakened to himself as an individual over against the family. It is here that the difference occurs between the Indian and the western family. For the western family is created by the consent of two individuals. It is not an arranged marriage. It is an association of individuals rather than an original primary group. It, therefore, tends to a greater sense of personal responsibility and, consequently, enhances initiative and human dignity. It is these qualities which enter into the kind of transformation of culture which is necessary to a humanistic modernization, and is reflected in the new literature, music and drama which is being produced there.

On the other hand, John Taylor,[14] is of the opinion that in the transformation from the primal vision of undifferentiated unity into that in which it is broken up by the self-awareness of individuals, a great sacrifice has been made of something essential to religion. He thinks the loss of the numinous and the unity of man with God and creation is a religious liability. This would be true if religion consisted exclusively of the feeling of the numinous and the sense of mystical unity conveyed by a culture, a truth which we should not, however, lose sight of. On the other hand, Christianity's emphasis is not mainly on this religious feeling but on the direct relationship of the individual with God to whom he is responsible as a person under moral obedience. This is what Von Oppen insists upon as essential to Christianity, and this is what distinguishes it along with Judaism from the mystical religions of the East and the more primitive nature religions. It is this which makes justice and an emphasis on human dignity of paramount importance for Christianity. This, therefore, constitutes the reason why Christians have to work for a transformation of cultures which obscure human individuality and personality. However, John Taylor is quite right in emphasizing the religious base of human life. Without it the value of personality itself is endangered. Man needs, therefore, to carry over the religious dimension into the transformed culture.

The second characteristic of most non-western cultures is what Van Leeuwen has decribed as ontocracy. By an ontocratic culture he means one in which nature is invested with divinity. In this type of culture the distinction between God and nature is obscure. Nature, being sacrosanct, is untouchable by technology and its mysteries must not be uncovered by science. The effect of onto-cratic culture is to produce a fatalism towards nature and to perpetuate social stagnation. Economic and social modernization become impossible wherever such a culture is consistently applied. It is this which is largely responsible for the description of the East as changeless. There the world is equated with nature and no sense of movement is felt towards a historical destiny, since the world is not looked at under the dimension of a meaningful history which man helps to create. In this culture change does not occur because the naturalistic fatalism implicit in ontocracy does not allow free-dom for man. He is, therefore, unable to determine his own future and break away from natural necessity to make for himself a historical destiny.

However, the introduction of modernism into eastern societies in the form of technology and industry has had the effect of creating a new sense of freedom from the domination of nature. The fatalism of the past is being overcome by a new feeling of historical destiny which man can create for himself through the freedom which he has begun to exercise. A transformation is taking place in the culture of the East at the point of human freedom with incalculable effects for the future. In this freedom eastern man will not continue to be satisfied with the poverty and degradation which his past fatalistic culture has imposed upon him. He will demand justice and a part in the decisions which determine his destiny and the destiny of the world. It is transformation of culture in this sense which calls for the encouragement of the Christian church, since it makes possible a demand from within the culture itself for justice, and a recognition of human dignity, and does not negate the positive elements of that culture. It enables them to take new expression.

An interesting instance of cultural transformation made necessary by the modernizing process comes from the literature of India. It was remarked upon by Dr Radhakrishnan in a talk to an all-India drama seminar, that in the past India never produced tragic plays. With the new sense which man has acquired in India that he controls his own destiny and the consequent idea of a purposeful goal to which he is moving, it is possible for tragedy to be written. For tragedy has meaning only in respect of purpose, since it happens when human purpose is defeated. M. M. Thomas[15] mentions the difference between the old poet Kalidasa's *Sakuntala*, which depicts not tragedy but the play of fate with a happy ending, and the modern Indian play-writers who are writing tragedies in regional languages.

To sum up, transformation of culture takes place through the realization of individual personality previously concealed by the sense of undifferentiated unity which characterizes non-western cultures, and through the development of the freedom of the human personality to create his own destiny. When these take place from within the culture itself, we can say that the basis for transformation is laid which will preserve cultural continuity. Where these are imposed, or are manifestations of western culture accepted or assimilated by groups or individuals within non-western cultures, then no real transformation of the original culture can take place. A cultural conflict arises and the support from within the culture itself for modernization and development is lost. However, cultural transformation must be controlled by human values belonging to the culture and sanctioned from beyond itself. It must not be finally determined by economic values alone.

So we come to the third question which is raised by culture and modernization. How can this transformation through personal awareness be promoted? This has been one of the most crucial issues facing the leaders of the Third World who realize that development, if it is to be successful and salutary, must be rooted in the culture of the people themselves. This is the point at which to mention the movement which is winning wide acceptance in many developing countries. It is the movement to create self-awareness among the people so that they become conscious of themselves as individual persons and exercise their freedom in the secular world which is growing around them. We shall try to explain this movement as part of the education process which is being promoted in many of the developing countries. We shall deal with this question in the next chapter.

NOTES

1. With apologies to an article in *Frontier*, Vol. 13, No. 1, February 1970.
2. See T. F. Torrance, *Theology in Reconstruction*, SCM Press 1965, pp. 14ff., quoted in B. N. Y. Vaughan, *Structures for Renewal*.
3. Quoted by Takeda Cho in 'The Ideological Spectrum in Asia', in *Man in Community*, p. 86.
4. In the second volume of their *History of East Asian Civilization*, entitled *East Asia: The Modern Transformation* (1965), quoted in C. E. Black, *The Dynamics of Modernization*, p. 196.
5. See op. cit., p. 9.
6. See 'The Ideological Spectrum in Asia', article by Takeda Cho, pp. 84ff.
7. See Kwame Nkrumah, *Consciencism*, pp. 66, 67.
8. Quoted in Gunnar Myrdal, *Asian Drama*, p. 772, from Shriman Narayan Agarwal, *A Plea for Ideological Clarity*, Indian National Congress, New Delhi 1957, pp. 9-10.
9. See *A Historian's Approach to Religion*, OUP 1956, and other works.
10. See 'Modernization of Traditional Societies and the Struggle for a New Cultural Ethos', article in *The Ecumenical Review*, Vol. XVIII, No. 4, Oct. 1966, p. 436.
11. See Kenneth Kaunda, *After Malungushi*, East Africa Publishing House 1969, p. 18; 'In Zambia every Zambian's contribution must ultimately be for the benefit of man'; and Mahatma Gandhi, *An Autobiography*, p. 299, where he explains *Sarvodaya*, his idea of human equality and welfare.
12. *The Dynamics of Modernization*, p. 81.
13. See *Man in Community*, pp. 236ff.
14. See *The Primal Vision*.
15. Art. cit., p. 431.

7

Self-awareness - Education for Development

The recent Asian Ecumenical Conference for Development[1] held in Tokyo in July 1970, reported that the new society which Asia needs 'will not come through the transformation of structures alone. It will come in large measure through a new kind of man whose will and attitudes and hopes will be geared to the vision of a new society'. With these words one of the most important regional conferences organized by SODEPAX identified the mechanism which must be motivated before development can really take place. It is the human persons who make up the developing societies who must be given a vision of a new society and a new awareness of themselves as the creators of that society. It means that the culture which forms their attitudes and consciousness has to be transformed at those points where this new vision and awareness can take hold of their mind and soul.

The whole passage deserves recording here because it forms a good introduction to the process of education by which this transformation can be effected, and because it comes from within the Third World itself:

Cultural transformation involves changes in the sentiments, values, habits and customs of human beings who have to adjust, as individuals and communities, to the demands of modernization in all fields of human endeavour. This dynamic process is an essential ingredient in human development. There is a vital role for education in achieving this purpose for, ultimately, it is through education that the human individual can become aware of himself as a person in a community of other persons. Through education he discovers his historical world and his tasks and responsibilities therein. More exactly, he discovers that his world is his responsibility and his task. Indeed, development is nothing more and nothing less than man transforming his world and, in such wise, transforming and elevating the quality of this life.

Education should not be construed narrowly to mean only formal schooling. We believe that programmes of training and formation, leadership development, channels of communication, such as mass media, can all lead to self-discovery and community action and thus are properly considered as other forms of education.

We recognize the importance to the masses of people in the Asian continent of the stress that has been put on the changing of economic and social structures which hinder the development of individuals and communities. But a society based on freedom, interdependence and mass participation in decision-making will not come through the transformation of structures alone. It will come in large measure through a new kind of man whose will and attitudes and hopes will be geared to the vision of a new society.

What Asians say about themselves and their need of an informed awareness of their responsibility for the development process and of themselves accepting the tasks which it imposes, is echoed in the experience of most of those who are sensitive to the faults and obstructions to a healthy social and economic growth in the Third World. Development which is imposed from outside or promoted by people who are not indigenous to the culture, or are not radically affected themselves by the changes and can opt out at any time, invariably reflects not the basic needs and convictions of the community itself but of the places from which its promoters came. The long and short term social and cultural effects of a particular programme of development are more likely to be anticipated by those who have to live with them than by those who have no personal stake in the community itself. It is for this reason, as well as because the local person is intimately related to the culture, that one of the primary needs of development is that it should be done by the people who belong to the community where it is going to take place, and that they should be aware of their responsibility and be inspired by a vision of a new society in terms of the culture which is meaningful to them.

This is why much attention is being given in the Third World to the means and methods by which self-awareness can be created among the people. Chile, Tanzania, Brazil, China and Ghana under Nkrumah, are the countries where attempts have been most intense to promote the process of self-awareness. The Spanish word *conscientizacion* has come to be widely applied in this process and is a word that was originally used in Latin America. The Portuguese word used in Brazil is *conscientizacao*. The expression used by

President Nyerere of Tanzania is 'education in self-reliance'. Nkrumah's 'consciencism', on the other hand, is to be understood in the light of his political ideology to which we shall turn attention in the next chapter.

Conscientizacion has to be understood as an education method which is accommodated to the need to enlist the conscious support of people in the development process. It is, therefore, adapted to the cultural situation of the people where it is promoted in the interests of political, economic and social change necessary to development. It varies, however, in its application not only according to the culture, but also the political situation, and can be used either by those in power or by those who seek to change the political *status quo*. It is, therefore, a highly ambiguous description and evokes differing reactions.

A vivid description of a government's reactions caused by an attempt by others to apply this method comes from the Dominican Republic.[2] It is an account of an attempt by a group of Dominican and Canadian youth to assist a peasant community at Sabaneta de Yosica to improve their lot. The plan consisted of a health, agricultural and co-operatives programme together with exercises in *conscientizacion*. This was to be the main effort and

> apart from the courses laid down by the government's education department, efforts would be made to present the peasants with the truth of their situation and to encourage them to seek possible alternatives. Political education of the peasants would not take the form of following one particular party, but rather of restoring their ability to make decisions.

As a result of the programme much progress was at first registered, and the peasants were able to set up a consultation of their own in which they proposed to discuss 'The social situation of the peasant'; 'The peasants' right to the land'; 'Land ownership the basic problem'; 'Union and unionization of the peasants'; 'Agrarian reform', and so on. This, however, drew the wrath of the government upon it and several of the peasants were arrested and the project had to be abandoned. *Conscientizacion* had been used to awaken people to their lot under the ruling government.

This incident serves to illustrate not only the end which *conscientizacion* is designed to serve, but also its meaning, the way it works and its problems. The basic meaning of *conscientizacion*, of course, is to make people aware of themselves as individual persons. This implies helping them to break away from traditions, fears and allegiances which keep them in economic poverty and social stagnation. It is a liberating exercise which works through educating people about themselves and about their condition. It produces

free individual persons who are willing and able to take action
about the condition of their life. This, then, is the original purpose
of *conscientizacion*, namely, to liberate people for action by giving
them a sense of themselves and of their situation. It serves a need
in the developing societies by arousing a sense of dissatisfaction
with underdevelopment and poverty and of freedom and ability to
change that situation. *Conscientizacion* as a philosophy and
methodology of education is a profound attempt to meet the need
for education for development. Its stress on self-awareness and self-
discovery of the processes of change relevant to a given community
is a liberating force in itself.[3]

An evaluation of *conscientizacion* will soon be needed and
SODEPAX has been requested to undertake this exercise. Like all
other things, it is liable to abuse and its sphere of application
requires to be described. Its value seems to lie in its liberating
effect and in helping people to assert their human dignity. It also
creates a revolutionary possibility in societies which are politically
and economically unjust or stagnant. On the other hand, it seems to
have some limitations. For while 'conscientizacion' creates a sense
of dissatisfaction and makes people aware of their personal and
social conditions, it does not itself prescribe any course of action
to remedy that situation. The immediate effect, therefore, of exercises in this process is not necessarily constructive unless it is tied
to a political programme. In fact it can lead to aimless dissatisfaction.

This exposes another limitation. It is that it is impossible to
dissociate this process of education from certain ideological presuppositions wherever it is related to a political and economic context. People become aware of themselves and of their society only
against the background of ideals which contrast with their present
condition. This is the reason why it is important to assess the
ideologies of development as much as the process of liberation set
in motion by *conscientizacion*.

Because *conscientizacion* labours under this limitation, it has
come to be used in conjunction with more positive aims, and is often
used as an adjunct of 'formation'. For whereas *conscientizacion*
itself is simply a means of liberation and creating self-awareness,
'formation' is a process of training whereby people are given certain
attitudes, habits and convictions which are appropriate to a particular policy, belief or ideology.

The 'consciencism' of Nkrumah which we shall consider in the
next chapter is such a harnessing of conscience or awareness to a
particular ideology. He proposes to harness the awakened African
conscience about itself to his own particular brand of socialism,
which he claims has its roots in the depths of African egalitarian

culture. It must, of course, be recognized that Nkrumah's 'consciencism' is more of a philosophical ideology arising out of African history and culture than a process which activates people through exposure to situations. It is geared to his own political policy which seeks to create African consciousness but does not welcome political participation. He says:

> Such a philosophical statement will be born out of the crisis of the African conscience confronted with the three strands of present African society. Such a philosophical statement I propose to name philosophical consciencism, for it will give the theoretical basis for an ideology whose aim will be to contain the African experience of Islamic and Euro-Christian presence as well as the traditional African society, and, by gestation, employ them for the harmonious growth and development of that society.[4]

In a different way the awakening of the conscience of the Chinese through the cultural revolution guided by Mao Tse-Tung is designed to serve his Marxist ideology. According to his thought, the political and economic revolution in China has to be sustained and continued by a conscience which is permanently aware of the social and economic facts calling for ongoing revolution. The Marxist revolution begun by Chairman Mao must not be allowed to settle down to a *status quo* in which privileged old revolutionaries become reactionaries. It must continue through the awakened conscience of the people concerning the objectives of the original revolution. This accounts for the particular brand of *conscientizacion* in modern China.

Conscientizacion is to be distinguished from what is generally known in the English-speaking world as adult education. For it is designed to meet the particular cultural and political situation of people whose social and economic context needs to be changed. It is used not simply to educate people culturally but to produce action which will change the situation and enlist participation.

> It is not simply a question of teaching the illiterate to read. They must also be sensitized to their situation which will stimulate in them the desire to change ... This education should take the form of training for a particular trade or profession, supplemented by political training in the relationships between social groups and the need for forms of government that encourage the creation of economically viable regions where rural and urban districts can exist side by side.[5]

It is, in fact, designed for economic and social development. In the hands of the government in power it is used to induce participation through creating awareness in the people of their world and its possibilities and of themselves. In the hands of the revolutionaries it becomes an instrument to persuade people of the political and economic structures which obstruct development and of their ability to change them.

It is in this light that the World Council of Churches sees Development Education, which is conceived to have two principal aims[6]:

1. To change the way of thinking and the traditional attitudes that produced and maintain current injustices both between and within nations. In other words, to foster an awareness of the causes of poverty and stimulate a search for ways of combating it at international and national levels; to call into question the present power structures; to create the will to bring about changes which will promote greater justice and freedom; and to fight against the ruling forces which wish to maintain the privileges they now enjoy;

2. To train men capable of promoting change, who would be able to detect the key problems and find concrete solutions. This means education should stimulate talents and creativity. It should expose the alienation inherent in certain educational systems aimed at conforming with the past and adjusting people to the *status quo*. It should encourage systems seeking to develop people as individuals, preparing them to serve the community as responsible citizens.

'Development and social change are set in motion not only by the autonomous processes of science and technology, but are subject to the conviction and aspiration of men,' says the report of the Montreux Consultation entitled *Fetters of Injustice*.

In line with this kind of thinking about relating education to the needs of development which has been promoted by the Commission on Education of the World Council of Churches and the World Conference on Christian Education and by UNESCO, is the recommendation of the annual meeting of the General Committee of SODEPAX.[7]

Within the structures of formal education at every level, and in the field of leadership development or formation, there are innovations and experiments taking place. SODEPAX should find ways to co-operate and participate in these efforts in so far as they relate to its mandate. SODEPAX should support those educators who are experimenting with methods of education aimed at stimulating social change, and fostering human development.

It goes on to contrast these methods with the traditional patterns of education 'in which the learners are not free to explore their own solutions to the problems created by the realities of their day to day life'.

In fact there has been considerable reaction in recent years against the traditional methods of education and against much that goes under the title of formal education. One of the centres from which this movement reacting against older western methods has received its direction is the Documentation Centre[8] in Cuernavaca in Mexico. At the time of writing a protracted series of conferences is going on at the Centre in which the issues raised by the problematic relevance of traditional methods to Latin America are being discussed. The fact that a stream of educationists is attending this series is in itself testimony to the concern which is being felt in circles which are involved in education and the development needs of Latin America.

The prime mover in this movement is Monsignor Ivan Illich, the Director of the Centre, well-known in Latin America and the USA because of the differences he has had with the Roman Catholic authorities as a result of his radical views on the celibacy of the clergy and on the presence of North American personnel and aid in Latin America. His tract, *The Seamy Side of Charity*, drew attention to this controversial champion of Latin American culture whose brilliance and sympathetic approach to their situation has been able to commend him to the *avant-garde* in Latin America in spite of the fact that he is Viennese born and now a US citizen. His special interest has been education. He was at one time Rector of the Catholic University in Puerto Rico. The theory for which he is now best known is that the traditional structure of education should be changed in developing countries on the grounds that it fails to educate the mass of the people. In an area where resources in personnel and money are limited, he holds that the present system of graded education over a period of years with examinations set at each level limits the availability of this privilege to a few and leaves the masses illiterate. It is loaded also with material which is of little use to the development needs of Latin America and could be eliminated even from formal education. What is the point of learning about European geography when the people do not even know their own country? He therefore calls for an education system which will be geared to the practical needs of the society and will be available to all. This, he claims, can be done through brief intensive periods of instruction which can be made available to the masses in smaller but more effective doses. He also demands methods which will enable people to learn through their own culture instead of methods in which foreign culture is inbuilt and where there is much teaching but little learning.

'De-schooling' and 'de-colonizing' of education are descriptions which convey the meaning of this movement very well. Shortly, an important conference is to be convened in Peru by the World Council of Christian Education at which some of these issues will be discussed, with the theme 'New Perspectives in Christian Education'[9] – a title which would have been improved by making 'Christian' qualify 'Perspectives' instead of 'Education'. One of the chief speakers will be Ivan Illich, which suggests the objectives of the conference.

The dissatisfaction which is widely felt in developing countries with traditional forms of education seems to be based, in fact, on three issues, each of which is reflected in one form or another in the experience of many in the developed countries themselves.

The primary cause of dissatisfaction is the alienation which is caused by the education which was introduced during the colonial period and has become the accepted medium in most of these countries. It is based on western values and, in addition, has inbuilt into it attitudes towards local culture which discourage any appreciation of it or of the history of the people and their society. The standards set by it are those which belong to the West. The effect is to alienate the educated groups from the masses of the people and their culture.

Types of education based entirely on western models, turn out graduates alienated *vis-à-vis* their own people and culture and *vis-à-vis* the particular manpower needs of their community, thus bringing about the problems of élitism, of the 'educated unemployed', of the brain-drain.

The underlying philosophy of education is oriented mainly towards the individual self and self-achievement rather than towards service and community responsibility.[10]

One of the most potent agents of alienation is usually thought to be the perspective from which the history of the peoples in developing countries is written. During the colonial period this history was written by historians who came from the colonial metropolis and had little sympathy or understanding of the culture and the other factors which went to create that history. It was measured by the standards of the West and consequently was radically devalued. This western bias in the writing of the history of colonial people has produced a strong reaction among scholars in developing countries who have set out to tell the story of the past from their own perspective with a deeper sympathy and understanding of the meaning of the culture and the history they describe.

Kwame Nkrumah, writing on this subject, echoes the feeling of people not only in Africa but many other parts of the Third World when he says:

> The history of Africa, as presented by European scholars, has been encumbered by malicious[11] myths. It was even denied that we were a historical people. It was said that whereas other continents had shaped history, and determined its course, Africa had stood still, held down by inertia; that Africa was only propelled into history by the European contact. African history was therefore presented as an extension of European history ... In presenting the history of Africa as the history of the collapse of our traditional societies in the presence of the European advent, colonialism and imperialism employed their account of African history and anthropology as an instrument of their oppressive ideology.
>
> Earlier on, such disparaging accounts had been given of African society and culture as to appear to justify slavery, and slavery, posed against these accounts, seemed a positive deliverance of our ancestors. When the slave and slavery became illegal, the experts on Africa yielded to the new wind of change, and now began to present African culture and society is being so rudimentary and primitive that colonialism was a duty of Christianity and civilization ... Our highly sophisticated culture was said to be simple and paralysed by inertia, and we had to be encumbered with tutelage ... In the new African renaissance, we place great emphasis on the presentation of history. Our history needs to be written as the history of our society, not as the story of European adventures. African society must be treated as enjoying its own integrity; its history must be a mirror of that society, and the European contact must find its place in this history only as an African experience, even if as a crucial one.[12]

When the history of a people is presented in terms which disparage their culture, their confidence in themselves and in their origins is broken. Compared with a culture which is held up as superior, it is very difficult for students to identify themselves with their own people in terms of such a devalued culture. Not only is an emotional difficulty created by the persuasion that their own culture is inferior, but they are in the process of education in terms of the so-called superior culture, acclimatized to think and act in its way. This is the alienation. It is both emotional and cultural. It is about this alienation that the French-Caribbean, Frantz Fanon, writes deprecating the way in which people of African descent like himself fall for the attractions of European standards and values. When people and, in particular, leaders of developing countries, are alienated in this way from the culture of their own people, they fail to identify with the motive forces within that culture from which alone development can derive its ultimate strength and support.

Alienation of this kind is not confined to developing countries. It happens also inside the developed world through the education process. Young people are alienated from the older generation by the kind of intellectual culture that is implicit in modern scientific technological education. They acquire a sense of superiority from this kind of education which devalues the culture of the older generation because it is less scientific and technological. Similarly, sons of working-class families tend to get alienated from their fellows by the higher education which they may win or enjoy. This kind of alienation has the effect of disqualifying and cutting off the alienated from participation and leadership among those to whom they originally and really belong. Translate this experience into terms of the circumstances of developing countries and you will have some idea of what alienation means for them.

The second cause of dissatisfaction with traditional forms of education inherited from the West is its irrelevance. The emphasis laid upon the academic side by this type of education is believed by many to deprive the student of the equipment which he needs for the modern technological age and is largely irrelevant. Why spend so much time and energy teaching the grammar of a language, or geography, to someone who is going to be a garage mechanic or a hotel waiter? However, this takes the objection too far. For the garage mechanic has to be able to read instructions on the manual and converse intelligently with his customer and employer, and the hotel waiter has to write out the bill intelligently and answer questions about the places from which the tourist comes or which he intends to visit.

Nevertheless, the weighting of formal education on the academic side places limitations on the demands of development in a technological age. Two things are, therefore, needed in the developing countries. The first is a greater emphasis on technical and vocational education at all levels. It is only in so far as there is an indigenous supply of techniques, managers and specialists that the development process can be successfully continued in the Third World. Dependence on foreign technicians and management distorts the process and has inevitable social and economic effects, such as we have already considered. The second thing needed is to fit the new technology into the culture of the area. Science and technology, particularly if they are in the hands of people who do not belong to the culture, invariably introduce cultural and social forces which contradict the local and national culture of the countries of the Third

World. The reconciliation of technology to this culture is, therefore, a primary need of the education process.

Adjustments from classical types of education to vocational and technical training have caused expenditure on education to rise to tremendous proportions. Economic factors are conditioned by political issues and the great drive for more and more education has placed many governments in an embarrassing financial position ... But, beyond the economic problem there is the cultural crisis caused by the introduction of educational methods and curricula that do not fit into the changing social patterns. Reconciling the need for knowledge, science and technology, to the important task of preserving concern for cultural and human values is a real challenge to the churches. SODEPAX should use the many studies already produced to encourage a serious attempt to solve some of these problems that make up the world educational crisis.[13]

The third cause for dissatisfaction with traditional forms of education has to do with methodology. Educational methodology is concerned with two issues. Chiefly, it is with the way in which people learn. But it is also concerned with the practical application of what is learned, the relation of the student to life. Traditional forms of education have derived their methods of teaching from the authoritarian context of political and social life. This is true not only of colonial situations, where it was assumed that what was taught would be accepted on the authority of the teacher in the same way as colonized subjects obeyed their masters, whether the obedience was willing and whether the teaching was assimilated or not. It has also been true of western education until comparatively recently that teaching was presented as information conveyed on the authority of the teacher. It was memorized in the belief that it was true, and the student was examined on his knowledge of these facts. The educational revolution, which has now taken place in the West itself under the influence of the scientific method of learning whereby people learn through experiment and assimilate through experience, has been happening also in the developing countries. But it has been for other reasons as well. The era of independence has started a reaction against authority and this has had an effect on education methodology. The experimental approach to learning has been assisted by the sense of freedom and responsibility for their political and economic destiny in many areas of the Third World.

This accounts very largely for the student revolution, not only in the West but in the developing countries also. It is a protest against traditional methods of conveying knowledge in universities and schools. Students are no longer content to sit down under the authoritative voice of their lecturer. The climate of freedom in which they now live creates a resistance to accepting what he says. They want to learn for themselves in the same way that the scientist learns from his experiments, particularly through discussion and projects. The teacher can be a resource person, if you like, and woe betide him if he has not got his facts straight!

But there is more than this which is in common between the student world of the West and the developing countries. They are both concerned about the practical application of what they find to be true. Facts have been revealed to them not only through the natural sciences but also through the social sciences, and they are aware of techniques by which change can be effected or, at least, can be attempted. In any case, there is the urge to test the truth of what they have learned by practical experiment. In the developing countries their concern is about development, justice and liberty. The education process, therefore, cannot any longer take place without involvement in the quest for a better world. It is there that the learning takes place, in the practical application of it, where the student explores his own solutions to the problems created by the realities of his day-to-day life.

While all this is true of the changing approach to education, the hard facts impress upon us the need also for a wider application of this approach in many parts of the world in order to accelerate development. Gunnar Myrdal, in his exhaustive study of South Asia, has drawn attention to this need. He says:

No independent value attached to education is considered to be valid if it conflicts with the value of education as an instrument for development.

From a development point of view, the purpose of education must be to rationalize attitudes as well as to impart knowledge and skills. In the South Asian countries, which have largely been stagnant for a long time and where attitudes antagonistic to development have taken firm root and become institutionalized, the changing of attitudes requires far greater emphasis than in the developed countries, where attitudes are already more rational, and are adjusted to permit further rapid progress. This is one of several reasons why educational reforms in South Asia have to guard against a tendency to adopt uncritically the education practices and policies of the western countries. If present educational practices and policies in the western countries should not set the pattern for South Asia, neither should the long journey by which those countries reached their present positions set the pace. The South Asia countries must strive for a much speedier dissemination of the attitudes, knowledge and skills favourable to development.[14]

He says this because his studies, like those of so many others who have examined the causes of underdevelopment, have led him to the conviction that the effectiveness of development policies depends in the long run on the attitudes of the people themselves. These attitudes can only be changed by a new approach to education and a more vigorous application of it.

In the writings on development problems of underdeveloped countries, it is a commonplace to acknowledge that a close relationship exists between the effectiveness of development policies in the economic field and prevailing attitudes and institutions. But it is fair to say that almost all economic studies of these problems, whether by South Asia or foreign economists, imply an almost complete neglect of this relationship and its consequences.[15]

A sad comment, but very true! The burden of what we have been saying so far is that development cannot be successfully promoted in the Third World unless it is undertaken and guided by the people themselves and unless it finds support from within their own culture. Again, for this to happen a new form of education has to be used. However, while stressing the importance of the indigenous effort and the self-reliance which is essential to any progress in development anywhere, and the education process which promotes the proper attitudes, we have to give due weight to the fact that healthy development cannot be fully achieved without reference to the global context which affects the development of all nations. We live in an interdependent world where the developed and the developing areas cannot contract out of the consequences of the technology which has made them neighbours who need one another. No doubt a certain measure of economic and social progress can be made in isolation. But it will bear the signs of isolation upon it, and it will detract from the prosperity and welfare of the whole with which every part is ultimately bound up.

This does not mean that the developed countries should undertake the task of development in the Third World. Everything we have said so far suggests that this does more harm than good, because the interests and perspectives of those who do the work inevitably colour or distort the results. What it means is that it is necessary for the developed nations to acquire a particular attitude towards the less affluent nations which are endeavouring to promote development from within their own resources – an attitude which will enable and encourage them to continue. It also means that they must acquire an awareness and become sensitive to the issues which bear upon the development of other peoples as well, of course, as upon the highly questionable form of society which they themselves have built up or are striving to correct.

This requires not only that education should be promoted in the developing countries to facilitate their development, but that this should be done within the developed countries also. There is a great need for a deeper consciousness in the richer countries of what development really means and what is needed to promote healthy growth. The debate on development needs to be promoted, extended and deepened with a view to exposing those with a limited view to the broad implications of integral human development on a world scale.

But the conceptualization of development depends on more than exposure to the views of others. It can only arise out of the realities which people now face in their daily existence when these are seen within the context of the whole human family. Since the content of the education process depends on the formulation of clear objectives, it is important that SODEPAX project from an international level the criteria by which such objectives could be determined. Illustrative of this need is the dilemma faced in the USA by the advocates of participation in world development. The American public must first come to a conceptual understanding in their own situation of what development is, for whom it is proposed, and what are its goals in specific areas of the world.[16]

Understanding what development really means is, I believe, the primary need for any kind of participation in this process wherever it takes place. For this, not only is it necessary to know the laws which govern social and economic change, to appreciate the local situation with its particular culture, and to see this from a global perspective, but also to realize something about man's nature and destiny – what is essential to humanity – and to view this in the light of what lies beyond man himself, transcends him and gives his humanity meaning.

Because of the importance of the proper understanding of development on the part of the developed nations and the need for their participation in the process along enlightened lines, much work has been done to outline the kind of education in development which should be promoted inside the richer nations. Much still needs to be done. In May 1969, an important consultation was convened by the World Council of Churches in Geneva[17] on Development Education, directed towards the responsibilities of the richer countries for world development. Its report sets out clearly the importance of realizing that the involvement of the richer countries must not be something that they would like to do, but a response that is demanded by the Third World and conditioned by the needs which the poorer nations themselves feel. For this response to be made it is necessary for the rich nations to be educated in the total situation of the poorer nations, their needs, their culture, their aspirations, their resources, their social and political background, as much as it is necessary for the developed countries to share their experience, skills and resources with the developing countries. A two-way education process must begin and each must listen to the other but, in particular, the poor nations must be heard and encouraged to speak. As a result of this dialogue, education material and relationships wherein education takes place can be gradually built up.

The report outlines several positive criteria which need to be observed in building up this education:

1. False images and myths about the developing countries must be eliminated. Response to need in the poorer countries has been evoked by presenting the people in a pathetic light. Dress, housing, habits, are portrayed as being primitive. This is deeply resented by the people who have a personal dignity and pride in their culture. For this reason people from the Third World should have a hand in the preparation of educational materials which are designed to tell the richer countries about themselves.

2. The message must be conveyed that true development is one which is initiated and directed by the people of the developing countries themselves. Nothing is resented more than policies and plans imposed and carried out from outside. Care must also be taken in what is called – rather questionably – 'joint planning', to avoid using superior wealth and techniques to steer the planning. Nothing gets the backs of people in developing countries up more than the arrogance of planners from outside. However right they may be – and they are not always right because there are many factors which they cannot appreciate in local situations – the fact that the initiative passes into their hands is deeply resented. Even if plans are mistaken, it is right to let people learn this for themselves as part of their own education.

3. The education process must be designed not simply to learn but to evoke an active, intelligent response.

4. The material must be accurate. Any description of the cultural, social and economic problems should be based on facts and data which are available from such agencies as FAO, UNESCO, UNCTAD, UNO and others.

5. The causes and the nature of world poverty should be truthfully explained as largely due to past exploitation by those nations

which are now wealthy, and the difficulties of disentangling the poor nations from the toils of colonialism, culturally and economically, should be stated clearly and honestly.

6. Development should be recognized as something more than economic prosperity and the social, cultural and spiritual underdevelopment of the rich countries should be acknowledged. Part of this spiritual underdevelopment is evidenced by the fact that rich societies are not concerned about the poverty and misery within the Third World.

7. The necessity for political action within the developed nations to induce greater concern and help for the developing countries must be faced, and this must be based on an accurate knowledge of the facts.

In addition to these recommendations from the WCC Consultation, there are two very important inter-related basic considerations which emerge from the Nemi report also. The first is that concepts of development vary according to the culture of the society in which they appear. The vision of the kind of man and society to which people aspire varies in different cultures. Out of these there arise different concepts of development. Now these concepts need to be changed. These can be changed by introducing to people within these cultures new perceptions of reality and new perspectives for changing the world in which they live. This change in perceptions and perspective happens when contact takes place with people of other cultures. For instance, people living within a traditionalist culture, where the world does not change and reality is perceived as static, acquire a new perception of reality when they meet people who perceive reality as changing and who by their action change society.

On the other hand, those who live within the other extreme – the technological culture – which is losing its hold on human values, need to be confronted with the perceptions of reality which will give them a new perspective on human and cultural values. This will tend to modify their concept of development in a human direction.

The content of the challenge and of the response comes in a large part from the process itself – as people help each other to achieve new understandings of other people and their communities, and as they achieve a mutual response to the human problems thus encountered.[18]

The other consideration related to this is that development education programmes should take account of issues arising out of regional differences. A programme adapted to one region may not be suitable to another. Issues vary from place to place and they need to be identified before a programme is applied. It is, therefore, necessary to develop a pluralistic approach in order to avoid the use of static and irrelevant methods.

NOTES

1. See *Liberation, Justice, Development*, p. 18.
2. See *Risk*, Vol. 5, Nos. 3/4, 1969, pp. 13ff.
3. *The Plenary Meeting* (The Nemi Report), p. 21.
4. *Consciencism*, p. 70.
5. See *This Month*, EPS, Oct. 1970, which describes the World Council of Churches' policy on Development Education.
6. Loc. cit., pp. 10, 11.
7. See Nemi Report, pp. 20ff.
8. Centro Investigaciones Culturales (CIDOC).
9. July 8-12, 1971.
10. See *Liberation, Justice, Development*, p. 19.
11. See *Consciencism*, pp. 62, 63.
12. 'Malicious' is an unfortunate expression as it implies ill-will. This is not true since the distorted record of African history is due to ignorance not ill-will.
13. Nemi Report, p. 20.
14. See *Asian Drama: An Inquiry into the Poverty of Nations*, p. 1621.
15. Op. cit., p. 1904.
16. See Nemi Report, p. 19.
17. See *Development Education*, WCC Report, 1969.
18. Nemi Report, p. 17.

8

Motivation - Ideologies and Development

The problem of providing motivation for the task of development has been felt by all political leaders in the Third World. Before development can successfully be undertaken people have to be persuaded to accept and participate in the changes which are needed for this to happen. This persuasion has to be backed by something more than an appeal to selfish interests and the profit motive. Since man is a rational and a moral being, he needs to be given an explanation of how and why changes must take place before he can be persuaded to participate energetically and responsibly in the development process.

The rational and moral explanation by which people have been engaged in this task is usually called an 'ideology'. As the word implies it means a system of ideas which are rationally co-ordinated to form a philosophy which attempts to explain things. The assumption made in the promotion of an ideology is that people are moved and that their behaviour is conditioned by the ideas which they assimilate. This understanding of the meaning of ideology, of course, is contrary to the Marxist use of the term. For Marxists and other economic determinists, an ideology is the opposite of this. For them it means 'ineffectual thought as opposed to causally efficacious behaviour'.[1] It refers in Marxism disparagingly to the false consciousness of an exploiting class used as a weapon against those dependent on them to maintain the *status quo*. However, as we shall see, Marxism itself is now commonly regarded as an ideology, in our sense of the term, on the grounds that its ideas have a motivating force because of the rational and moral explanation which it attempts to give of things.

For Christians the use of ideology to motivate action has posed the radical question of reconciling the ideological elements designed to induce this action with ultimate truth, since the ideology cannot itself also claim the authority of absolute truth. An ideology which claimed such an absolute status would be in radical conflict with the Christian faith itself since that faith alone is accepted in this sense by Christians. This, of course, was the conflict between Fascism and the Confessing churches of Germany during the second world war.

Ideology has, therefore, been a matter for debate among Christians because of the need which people – including Christians – feel of an ideological element in their thought to promote social change.[2] The question is whether ideologies can be reconciled with the absolute nature of Christian truth. This question was considered at the Geneva Conference on Church and Society. There H. B. Conteris of Uruguay said that ideologies are necessary to the self-awareness of the dispossessed and to their search for true humanity in political commitment. He said that established authorities do not need an ideology because they have power. It is different with the powerless and the poor. They need an ideological grasp of reality. Such an ideology explains and analyses history with the intention of showing where and how forces are working in the interests of liberation. It therefore shows where the poor can have hope.

This is in line with the prophetic interpretation of history whenever it is claimed that God is operating in a particular historical situation, as, for instance, in the liberating effects of technology and in political independence movements. Such an ideological interpretation always involves a risk of faith, that is believing that God is actually making the changes. But some claim that while such an ideology does call for a response of faith and does determine the actions of Christians in particular situations, yet the Christian knows that such an ideology is not absolute and that it is subject to correction and further development. The Christian knows that in such an ideology history is being looked at from a particular standpoint and involves a measure of distortion. Indeed, this distortion of history was regarded by Reinhold Niebuhr's *Moral Man and Immoral Society* as necessary because without it the poor and underprivileged would never get the courage and the rational purpose to change the situation in which they were enslaved. It is to see the truth through the only glasses that provide vision for the poor. This is a way of reconciling Christian faith and ideology, by recognizing the relative nature of an ideology and so, its distortion.

On the other hand, Ronald Preston[3] questions the validity of ideological motivation for moral action. He does, indeed, acknowledge that ideological elements are inevitable in all human thought. He also counsels us to become more conscious of their presence and to realize that we can never escape them. This is because we belong to our own culture. 'Pure thought' is impossible. But he says that this does not justify the cultivation of ideologies as a deliberate policy. He thinks we should be as non-ideological as possible in our practical decisions, 'as cool as a physician in a technological epidemic'. In this way, some of the irrational elements in political allegiance will be eliminated since politics will have the ideological dimensions taken out of it and with it those emotions which the reality of politics does not warrant. He says that politics will in this way be de-fused. He therefore thinks that it is the duty of Christians to show how change can be effected without cultivating ideological illusions to induce people to effect it. In holding this opinion Preston thinks he is in line with those who talk about the end of ideologies, an end which has been brought nearer by the disillusion caused by revolutions inspired by ideologies and even more by science and technology as opposed to ideologies. Science and technology, he says, are different from ideologies because they are pragmatic, pluralist, sceptical and aware of the complexities of the situation. Science and technology tackle individual problems rather than approach the whole situation with an answer derived from an ideology. Preston finds that what answers to this scientific approach is the Christian virtue of prudence, which is a safer guide than the fervour and conviction induced by ideologies. It is more in line with the knowledge which the Christian has that the kingdom of heaven will not be established by man within history, which is the belief engendered by ideological thinking.

The need to de-absolutize ideological formulations and at the same time to provide for the need for an ideological base in human thought by which to induce response to the demand for change, was considered by the group reporting on 'Theological Issues in Social Ethics' at the Geneva Conference.[4] It said:

By ideology we mean a process quite different from a total system of ideas which is closed to correction and new insight. Ideology as we use it here is the theoretical and analytical structure of thought which undergirds successful action to realize revolutionary change in society and to undergird and justify the *status quo*. Its usefulness is proved in the success of its practice. Its validity is that it expresses the self-understanding, the hopes and values of the social group that holds it, and guides the practice of that group. Its inner problem is its relativity to the power struggle of that group, and the danger of cynicism on the one hand and fanaticism on the other, when ideology's claim to be the truth for all men is challenged.

The relation of theology to the human situation offers help at this point. Theology reflects not only action but interaction between God's revelation and man's ideological understanding of his own condition and desires. Precisely in so far as the

Christian is serious in seeking and acting on the command of God, believing and proclaiming it to be such, he becomes open to the correction of God out of his experience. Christians, like all human beings, are affected by ideological perspectives. But their witness is the way in which they show themselves to be constantly corrected in their encounter with God and their neighbours while acting on their faith.

In other words, the report accepts the usefulness of ideology in view of the cultural conditioning of men in human society which demands an ideology relevant to their condition which will evoke the necessary response and sustain their action. Because of man's emotional nature ideologies give him a rational hope based on an interpretation of facts. An ideology is sufficient to engage his co-operation without claiming that ultimate status which leads to fanaticism. Indeed, it is when ideologies are not limited in their claims that development programmes based on them lead to disillusion and frustration. This is why it is important that ideologies should be both constantly under the criticism of ultimate truth and yet offer hope because they uplift men to see and grasp at their destiny within terms of their own culture.

The test of an ideology, however, is its practical application in developing situations. We shall, therefore, look at the uses to which ideologies are put, and then at the way in which they have worked out in certain practical circumstances.

There are two clearly identifiable uses which ideologies have served in developing countries. The first is the needs of nation-building and the second is the promotion of modernization. These two uses are usually inter-related, since nation-building must first take place before modernization can begin. Similarly, a measure of modernization is necessary to the task of nation-building. It is a manifestation of the interaction of politics and economics. So it is that speaking on 'Ideology, Politics and National Integration' at the Third Caribbean Scholars' Conference in Georgetown, Guyana, Professor Robert Anderson of the University of Puerto Rico[5] said:

> We assume that a country must enjoy at least a minimum measure of national integration before it can effectively develop or modernize. But the process of one tends to interfere quite directly in the process of the other.

Modernization makes nation-building possible, and nation-building facilitates modernization. It is impossible to separate the two processes and provide an ideology for nation-building which does not relate to modernization or *vice versa*. In fact, modernization adds new complexities to the task of nation-building which do not exist before the modernization process begins. For instance, the work of integration has to be extended and applied to new groupings which appear as a result of industrialization.

Thus the developing nation is faced with the pull of two kinds of disintegrative tendencies: first, the rivalries among traditional culture is to introduce a new concept. This is creolization. It is a class, or economic antagonism as industrialization and modernization progress. One might assume that where these two kinds of cleavages tend to re-enforce each other – where different ethnic or linguistic groups tend to engage in separate economic or social activities, e.g. as the Chinese in South East Asia or in the so-called plural societies of Africa – the obstacles to genuine national integration are complex and difficult indeed; and, on the contrary, that when economic cleavages cut across or overlap cultural or 'traditional' differences, the possibility of accommodative integration would be greater. Be that as it may, the point to emphasize here is that 'national integration' in today's developing countries includes not simply the process of 'primitive unification' ... but also the successive and simultaneous accommodation of new groups and institutions, created by the conscious commitment to modernization itself.[6]

Nevertheless, these processes, though inseparable, are distinguishable. With this qualification in mind we shall study them successively.

The need to build new national units arose with the passage from colonial to independent status. Under the colonial regime, nationhood would have impeded the machinery of government since it constituted a threat to the colonial power. It was essential to colonialism that the centre of power should remain in the colonial metropolis and that legislation which a nation normally makes for itself should be passed down from there. The essentials of nationhood were, therefore, withheld in the interests of direct government by the imperial power. What existed were merely the threads of a political entity, a geographical area, a dispersed system of administration, a social *élite* partial to the colonial power and, usually, a number of buildings which had been used centrally for administrative purposes. The people within the geographical area were separated into groups, ethnic, religious and cultural, with no co-ordination between them. In Africa, for instance, tribal groups within an administrative area retained their separate identity and in India the caste system was allowed to continue under the imperial regime.

With the advent of independence it was necessary for these geographical areas to become political units and to be welded into a nation. Nation-building at this point was, therefore, a political task. Its main endeavour was to integrate separatist groups into one political unit. The problem facing the nation-builder was to persuade the distinct units to accept central authority and to co-operate with it.

Now an analysis of political authority shows that it must be centred upon a set of values. This means that the task of commending authority depends largely upon getting people to accept and assimilate these values around which the society is organized.[7] In many developing societies, for instance in Africa and even in Latin America, these values are often neither clearly held nor consistently spread throughout the society. This means that authority and the instruments by which it is exercised have to be constantly created to face the forces of disintegration. It is here that the ideological task comes in. For ideology attempts to give political explanations of social realities. It does this by advancing theories of explanation, by slogans, and by the use of symbols such as national flags and colours, and national anthems. For this reason ideology has been defined as 'a comprehensive explanation of the present, an image of a desirable future state, and an explanation of the process by which the present can be transformed into the future'.[8]

The problem of authority, essential to political unification and integration, arises mainly, of course, when a society begins to move out of its traditional structure into the modern type of society. Traditional societies, in so far as they retain this character, have no need of an ideology to promote the values on which authority is built. For they are fused around these values already and remain unquestioned. Whether, in fact, there are any such societies is highly questionable because, as has often been observed, all societies have individuals who question the suitability of political institutions to social realities as they are or should be. All societies are 'prismatic' in this sense. But certainly, when the 'fused' traditional society begins to be differentiated and 'refracted' by the modernizing process, the value systems break up and political authority has to be rebuilt around values which are commended to the people. This is why ideology is thought to be a necessary programme in a developing society.

This, then, is how ideology serves the purpose of legitimizing authority and integrating societies around this authority. It does so in two ways, first, by binding the community together in a higher solidarity which can in turn form the moral basis for that society. This is the social function of ideology. But it also has an individual function in that it assists the individual to see his role in society. This function of assisting the individual to discover his identity is frequently overlooked, but is important because it creates intelligent commitment to development and acceptance of authority. In this way the political basis of a society is built up and nationhood begins to become a reality.

Ideologies, however, take their character very largely from the groups or the individuals which undertake the task of spearheading the building of the new nation. This is to say that their interests and perspectives are built into the ideology which they promote. Of these groups the most powerful agent is the political party. This is found in one of two systems – the multi-party political system or the one-party system. Within the multi-party system the political party normally shares certain basic values with the others which they promote in common. These include the democratic values as well as others. But their efficiency and integrative effect is limited by their lack of power. So it is that the multi-party system inherited from the West in most developing countries has given way in many countries to the one-party system as a more effective agent of political integration. In some situations the one-party system ought to be able to integrate the society much more effectively in the initial stages of political development than the multi-party system because it is able to concentrate on the task both of nation-building and modernization more intensively than separate political parties which have to watch their own interests and catch votes. But in particular it is thought sometimes to be more effective because it is able to harness to its purposes an ideology appropriate to the need and to its policy. It is, therefore, often considered to be a more effective mobilization system. The People's Convention Party of Ghana under Nkrumah was an instance of this. Similar systems have been effective in Mexico, Guinea and Mali.

This seems to be the secret of the Chinese revolution where the ideological element is more powerful than in any other developing situation. Leaving aside its defects, the creation of the new China seems to be backed by remarkable enthusiasm which has been engendered by the ideology promoted by this special Marxist brand of the one-party system. The possibility that here it may meet its nemesis does not detract from the fact that it has been an effective mass-mobilizer in the interests of nation-building.[9]

We have been looking at the part which ideology plays in nation-building and at the way it operates in mobilizing developing societies around sets of values which undergird political authority and give impetus from among the people to the development process. It will assist us to understand the role played by ideology and its limitations if we look briefly now at an issue which has been a concern of political scientists, particularly in the Caribbean.[10] It is that of the regional integration of existing, juridically distinct political units.

Nation-building has been undertaken in the independence era
on the supposition that each territory or country has the possibilities
of a viable economy. In the Caribbean it was assumed that this
viability would be assisted by Commonwealth trade relations and
other forms of assistance arising out of colonial connections. Each
territory, therefore, as it became independent framed its economic
policy to this continued dependent relationship on the ex-colonial
power. This sometimes took the form of a stream of delegations to
the home base requesting preferences and continued aid.

The 'beggar mentality' which this kind of dependence has fostered
is now the cause of considerable self-criticism and even, perhaps,
of disgust among self-respecting West Indians and other members
of the Caribbean community. Alistair McIntyre, writing on 'Decolonization and Trade Policy in the West Indies',[11] says:

> Uncharitable observers have gone as far as to characterize these
> territories as mendicant economies, which are always begging
> in the rest of the world for tariff preferences, for financial aid, or
> opportunities for emigration. For instance, journalists vie with
> one another in coining terms of opprobrium for West Indian
> delegations going abroad in search of economic assistance. One
> example of this was furnished by the London *Times* which
> described a recent West Indian delegation to London as a
> 'beggars' opera'.

This dependent economic relationship has been linked with a
cultural amalgam which reflects the situation where the poorer
separate countries look to the richer. Cultural ties follow economic
relations and are patterned by them. The films, the education, the
techniques, the manners build up the image of the mother country
and devalue the culture which belongs to the people of the Caribbean themselves. This is reflected very clearly in the way in which
the Creole culture which expresses the feelings and reminds the
people of their origins, is submerged and concealed beneath a
façade of European and now, of American culture. So little is
known or written about Caribbean culture, perhaps for this reason,
that it is worthwhile reproducing some things said by Professor
Braithwaite, who is a sociologist and is now the Pro Vice-Chancellor
of the University College of the West Indies in Trinidad, in an
address to a youth conference in Jamaica:[12]

> The best way perhaps to understand the nature of our own
> cultural, ethnic, or communal groups, and second, the growing
> process which took place in the Caribbean as a result of the
> presence in the area of two major cultural groups: the African
> (slaves) and the European (masters). What happened in this

geophysical situation was that although the Africans were brought as slaves and the whites were here as masters and they (the masters) evolved an ideology which said that the blacks were non-human, there still resulted an interaction between these two sets of people – a very important interaction – which came about as a result of physical contact, as a result of cultural contact. Each group was to some extent interacting with the other, and at the same time contributing something to the society as a whole. The Europeans contributed (basically) a social, economic and political framework, the plantation, with its machinery, its organization and its routine. At the same time, the African slaves contributed much more than labour because they were also contributing their (spiritual) culture which had in fact come with them from their ancestral continent. What they were doing was contributing dance, music, speech (the dialect which we still speak today as a result of that interaction of African languages with a European one) and social organization which to some people seem very fragmented but which was their response to their very peculiar situation. Creolization is the mixing and synthesizing of these two elements – the element of Africa and the element of Europe – in the Caribbean; and in the Caribbean these two elements became a very subtle and important mixture. But another thing to notice, however, was that because of the dominance of the master, of the European, only those elements of the local or creole culture which appeared to be European were acknowledged and respected, and those elements of the culture which were clearly black and African were submerged and put aside and ignored. It does not mean, however, that because we do not recognize it, a creole culture does not exist. If it did not exist, we would in fact have no meaningful society at all.

The culture of the Caribbean is, therefore, geared to a political and economic situation in which each territory looks away from the Caribbean itself towards the metropolitan powers, Britain, France, Spain, Holland, the USA. This disintegrated economy is now acknowledged to be an impossibility in the face of modern realities. The European Common Market alone is sufficient warning of the necessity for the Caribbean territories to turn away from the West and look towards one another and form closer economic links. This is now happening as a result of the formation of the Caribbean Free Trade Association which is enlarging the market of the separate territories and bringing in a measure of rational economic planning. Being only a Free Trade Association the integration is of a limited kind and does not require the surrender of any sovereignty on the part of the member territories, but only contractual agreements between them.

There are, however, a number of problems. Some of them are being resolved by negotiation and by the creation of the Caribbean Development Bank which is being financed by generous grants from outside. However, there still remains the problem of whether economic integration of this kind can produce the instruments to forge the whole into a more realistic political entity.[13] The interesting experiment of the West Indies Federation which broke up after only four years in 1962 because of political difficulties, some of them due to distrust and lack of adequate communication, was an attempt to face the political implications of economic necessities. For there is a *continuum* between political and economic integration. That is, economic integration generally requires nation-states to yield elements of national sovereignty at least in areas of economic decision-making. This political integration is

> a process whereby political actors in several distinct national settings are persuaded to shift their loyalties, expectations and political activities towards a new centre, whose institutions possess or demand jurisdiction over the pre-existing national states. The end result of a process of political integration is a new political community superimposed over the pre-existing ones.[14]

The new attempt at economic integration in the Caribbean is designed to rescue the region from its difficulties without political integration of any kind. Political leaders are aware of the limitations imposed by lack of political integration. The result is that a search is going on for a substitute which will assist the economic effort.

The most widely accepted of these is the identification of the common culture of the Caribbean. Much is being done, therefore, to create an awareness of this culture and to accept it consciously. To assist this, communications networks are being built up in the Caribbean in order to link the territories together by a common cultural identity. Films and radio talks about the separate territories are being made and recorded for distribution throughout the area to create understanding and break down inter-territory ignorance and prejudice. The University of the West Indies is one of the most effective agencies of this linking together of the scattered islands and mainland territories, not least because the future leaders themselves are being educated there rather than in Europe or North America.

The question, however, still remains whether the myth of Caribbean identity can be promoted, as an effective ideology, to bind the whole region of the Caribbean together, without the political instruments which are normally required to promote a myth which will be strong enough also to mobilize the effort needed for modernization and economic viability. A comparative study of the use of ideologies in other developing countries by Professor Anderson[15] leads us to doubt whether this is possible. For an ideology to mobilize the masses and integrate the people in a common effort in any area, a high degree of centralized policy and control is required, as the one-party system has proved in African territories and in Mexico. In the Caribbean the fissiparous forces which disintegrate the region are very strong indeed. One need mention only the cultural attachments to ethnic origins and colonial bases, to say nothing of the economic temptations offered by speculative investments and trade and aid relationships outside the area.

In these circumstances, can the ideological myth succeed? There are very few signs of its success at present. Possibly there will be greater progress when the decolonizing process has been completed and the links of dependence with Europe (and North America) are broken by the European Common Market. It is doubtful whether the Caribbean myth will stand the strains without political support. The Black Power movement itself, though it assists in some ways, destroys the power of the myth in other ways. This is for the simple reason that the peoples of the Caribbean are not all black nor all African in origin. They are also coloured, yellow and white. There are Indian, Spanish, French and Dutch areas which are necessary parts of the whole which is to be integrated. Not all are willing to accept a claim which is not, in any case, true of them all, that they have the same historical experience of slavery to bind them together and give meaning to the Caribbean identity ideology.

This poses the question, therefore, whether the Caribbean is not an area where 'the end of ideologies' might not be more profitably entertained. Would not the factor of self-interest be a more realistic motivation in the circumstances of the modern Caribbean? Perhaps what Ronald Preston says could be applied in this particular type of culture, which has a much higher degree of sophistication, making it more impervious to the ideological myth than many other developing areas; that is, that instead of ideological myth and instead of an interpretation of Caribbean history with a bias, it is better to emphasize the Christian virtue of prudence and the secular code of enlightened self-interest. It is not an easy question and should not even be answered by someone who has lived through the experience of the people and can fully sympathize, but by the people themselves and their leaders.

We now move on to consider the uses which ideologies serve in the promotion of modernization. In what follows we shall rely on Gunnar Myrdal's *Asian Drama*[16] which contains his remarkable

study in extent and depth of South Asia. A review article on the
book from inside the Indian scene[17] has shown up some of the
weaknesses of Myrdal's conclusions. In particular, the article questions whether Myrdal has done justice to the comprehensiveness
and complexity of the issue which he states. The issue played out
in the *Asian Drama* is the conflict between attitudes, institutions,
economic realities and demographic trends, on the one hand, and
the modernization and development goals of the nations in the
region on the other. His interpretation of the fundamental relationships and conflicts is, therefore, questioned. In particular Myrdal
is seen as looking at the situation from the point of view of the
possibilities offered by the westernized *élite*'s involvement in modernization without giving sufficient attention to the dichotomy between
them and the masses whose engagement in the process is still very
limited. With those limitations in mind, which are inevitable in a
Westerner, however able himself, writing about the East, we can
take Myrdal as a competent guide through the uses which ideologies have served in South Asia and relate what has taken place
there to what is happening in similar fields of development elsewhere.

Myrdal begins with a distinction between ideologies as debatable
theories which claim to explain realities on the one hand, and
ideologies as social facts which operate as agents by which policies
of development are directed or from which they emerge, on the
other. It is the latter with which he deals in his second volume.
He shows how they have been operated. He makes a comprehensive
survey of the development situation in South Asia as the countries
there seek modernization. He traces the way in which ideologies
play a part in the modernizing process and how the part varies in
different situations and according to the ideology used. As a sociologist he does not assess the ideologies for their truth value but only
discusses their effects and mode of operation as social factors. This,
in fact, is what we are concerned about in this chapter. It is not to
assess the truth of ideologies but to reflect theologically upon their
operation in developing situations and through this reflection to
make a moral assessment of the ideological movement as a whole in
development. Myrdal himself does not make this theological reflection but he supplies the material for such a reflection to be done by
Christian theologians.

Myrdal identifies four main ideologies which have operated in
the modernization of South Asia. These four are interconnected and
directly related to economic development as a primary end. They
are the ideology of planning, egalitarianism, democracy, and
socialism.

Planning can be understood to be an ideology in the sense that it contains an idea that promotes it. The idea is that development can be best promoted by means of a plan based on research and geared to accepted aims. Developing countries have all gone through this exercise of providing a plan by which their development will be attained. They have usually been limited to a five year period after which they have been reviewed and extended for a further period. That planning has an ideological appeal was illustrated in an amusingly meaningful incident after the General elections in Jamaica in 1962. Norman Manley's governing party had used the slogan of 'The Man with the Plan'. Manley's party, however, was defeated and the other party took over under Bustamante. It was said of him that on taking over the Prime Minister's desk he was found rummaging through the drawers. On being asked by his private secretary what he was looking for, he said, 'I am looking for the Plan'. Obviously, it was impossible to lay physical hands on the mystique supplied to Manley's personality by the ideology of planning with which his party had credited him.

The way in which Myrdal describes the same thing is by saying: [18]

Planning becomes the intellectual matrix of the entire modernization ideology ... Superficially at least, the planning ideology now rules supreme in the South Asian countries. It provides the terms of reference of much of public discussion of their social and economic issues – in the literature and press of these as of all other countries participating in that discussion, in the pronouncements of political and intellectual leaders, in the deliberations, assumptions ... These nations or those individuals in them who are at all articulate, are in various degrees becoming 'plan-conscious' and this is commonly asserted to be a good thing ...

It is not difficult to understand and feel the ideological appeal of planning. What is not so easy is to assess its actual performance and to uncover its pretensions. Of course, planning is good, but as an ideology its dangers must be recognized and its mode of operation examined. This is what Myrdal does in the Asian situation. For instance, Myrdal shows how assumptions about planning in South Asia can serve as a background for government intervention for political reasons.

Even when there is little actual planning, and still less implementation, the ideology of planning serves as a rationalization for interventionist practices ... every government wants to be able to claim large scale intervention as an accomplishment of planning for economic development, even when the planning and co-ordination have been very deficient. Every advance in the economy is presented as a result of successful planning. At the same time, the planning ideology gives a rationale for austerity and makes it more possible for the government to explain why living conditions are not improving.[19]

It is not that planning is an exercise that is unnecessary to development. It is that the ideological status which it acquires in South Asia and other developing situations introduces a new factor. That is, whatever is done in the name of planning is right, for the name of planning has acquired messianic status. On the other hand, in developed countries the ideological element is not present in the planning programme. In the Communist countries, where state planning originated, there is no need to promote the ideological element since popular participation is elicited by other means. In the western countries, where state planning has been introduced at a later stage of development,

> the impulses towards economic planning ... stem from this present life, not from an ideological tradition of policies that determined their early development. In state planning for economic development, the South Asian countries may not be so very different – at least, in intent – from the western countries today; but this similarity, so far as it exists, is precisely what represents the difference in initial conditions. And while some western countries play down what economic planning they have, and try to convince themselves that theirs is a 'free economy', the South Asian countries tend to play it up, and pretend that their planning amounts to much more than it does. They have accepted planning as an idea even before they are able to translate much planning into reality.[20]

The point is that the developing countries have to use planning as an ideology to promote development and even to initiate it, whereas the developed countries do not need the impulse of ideology because the process is well under way there. Other forces are at work in them which remove the need for the ideological element which is found in planning in the developing countries. Planning happens in the developed countries only at a later stage and then it is as a neutral un-ideological exercise because there is no need to use the idea of the 'plan' to mobilize popular engagement in the economic effort. In developing countries, the ideological element is needed to give the people the assurance that they are involved in a task which is rationally based on values and objectives which they are accepting or have already accepted. In any case, the ambivalence of this ideology of planning is reflected in its application to developing countries.

The second ideology to which Myrdal draws attention is that of equality. A comparable relation exists between the welfare state system in the West and egalitarian ideology in the East as exists between economic planning in the older countries and government planning in the developing countries. In the West the welfare state, in the same way as 'planning', has come into being after the development process has advanced both socially and economically to a point where egalitarian policies could be implemented. In fact, they had to be introduced at this point in the interests of economic growth and social harmony. It is true that socialism supplied some emotional support to it, but it was in fact the rational inference from economic, political and social premises which produced the welfare state. In the developing countries of which Myrdal has supplied evidence from Asia, particularly from India, egalitarianism was introduced from the West before the development process was effectively in motion, and was used as one of the motivating ideologies for development. It is in this context that we shall now again watch the ideological factor at work, in order to assess its place in development, taking our bearings from Myrdal's social and economic analysis of the Indian situation and the other South Asian countries.[21]

Egalitarianism was built into the constitution of India in 1950 and its Directive Principles. In 1956 Pakistan was committed to it. Similarly, Ceylon, though more quietly, Burma, Indonesia, Thailand, Malaya and the Philippines 'are also committed to principles of equality'. Stress was, therefore, laid in the plans, particularly the First Five Year Indian Plan, on the equalization of incomes and wealth and the more widespread ownership of the means of production. Subsequent plans reiterated this policy. What has happened, however, is that equalization has not taken place and in fact inequalities have increased in South Asia. This has led to a number of investigations in India, but without producing any effect, according to Myrdal and other observers. In other words, egalitarianism has remained a pure ineffective ideology which has proclaimed an ideal but has not been able to bring about its realization.

Myrdal's analysis leads us to infer again that the ideological element is too ambivalent to be always a reliable instrument in the service of development. His analysis shows how egalitarianism is manipulated by politicians as a myth in which they appear, indeed, to believe intensely but which they either do not seriously intend or are unable to implement in the face of the economic and social facts. The result is that the masses are spell-bound by a mirage of equality created by the promises of political speeches. Much is said about the 'welfare state' as if, because it is an ideal of the constitution, it were a reality.

Thus it is common to use the term 'welfare state' not just to indicate the type of society India aspires to be but to describe its present nature. Expressions such as 'a classless society' and a 'co-operative commonwealth' are frequently employed to describe the direction in which India is moving as a result of actual policies. Various verbal combinations containing the nuclear concept 'socialist' are also commonly used for that purpose, with stress laid on the implied element of equality. That India is in the course of an 'economic and social revolution' has become almost a commonplace public utterance. Naturally, this habit of speech engenders a certain amount of 'double-talk' in public discussion and a tendency to indulge in rhetoric isolated from reality.[22]

Myrdal gives causal explanations for this dichotomy between pretensions and achievements. He mentions the magnitude of the task of alleviating the lot of the poor as being so great and the conditions as so appalling that it is necessary for the people to live in a world of illusion created by the ideologies of change. He also mentions the callousness bred by years of familiarity with social suffering and poverty which removes the feeling of pity so essential to action by those in a position to get anything done. If Pope Paul had been born in India he would not have wept over its sufferings when he visited it. Myrdal also mentions the 'big business interests who provide the funds for political activity' and so prevent the implementation of policies of equalization while the myth keeps the people spellbound.

These are causal explanations for the failure to act which a social scientist is able to detect. The question which is raised concerning the ideology of egalitarianism is why is it not itself sufficient to move people in spite of these obstructions. This requires analysis by competent social scientists. Myrdal only gives a hint of what such an analysis might reveal. He distinguishes between the 'independent value' and the 'instrumental value' of equality. Equality has an independent value of its own, and this, of course, is the substance of the ideology itself. That is, it is good for people to be treated as equal and to have equal opportunities. This, however, is all that the ideology says. Equality, on the other hand, has an 'instrumental value' also with which the ideology has nothing to do. Its 'instrumental value' consists in the fact that an improvement in the social and economic status of people enables them to be more effective agents of development from which they, of course, in turn benefit. Equality provides not only an incentive to participate in development. It also enables people to be more effective participants in the process. Should it not, therefore, be considered and commended not simply as an ideology, but as an effective instrument of development? Myrdal gives instances from the Indian situation of ways in which inequalities hamper, and greater equality would assist, participation. He says:[23]

Levelling would have an instrumental as well as an independent value. For one thing, all the inequalities inherent in the traditional social stratifications – which we characterized as gross imperfections in 'free competition' ... are recognized as being obstacles to development. That caste in India is such an obstacle is obvious ... Since large numbers of labourers in agriculture and other occupations are despised as untouchables, the caste system fortifies the prevalent contempt and disgust for manual work. Since an orthodox Hindu regards not only those who perform this work but everyone outside his own caste as beyond the pale, it also warps and stultifies ordinary human feelings of brotherhood and compassion. It is clear and generally recognized that similar phenomena, including restrictions on women's rights, present in various forms and degrees in other South Asian countries, frustrate development.

On this question of the effect of economic, as distinct from social, inequality on the development effort, Myrdal recognizes the controversy that exists concerning the conflict between economic equalization and economic progress, and the claim that equalization has to be paid for by retarded progress. On the other hand, he says that detailed knowledge of the relation of these two aims is not available.

We lack detailed knowledge of how factors such as the savings ratio, labour input and efficiency react to different systems of distribution; discussion of these matters is abstract and speculative.

In South Asia the details are even more meagre. Then he says:

Nevertheless, it is possible to point to a number of conditions that suggest that there, much more than in western countries, an increase in equality would help rather than hinder development. He gives four considerations. The first is that a removal of economic inequality also removes social inequality which in South Asia is detrimental to productivity for reasons already given. The second is that economic deprivation by causing malnutrition is adversely affecting the labour input and efficiency, whereas better distribution of wealth will reverse this situation. The third is that in South Asia in the early stages of industrialization people with higher incomes indulge in conspicuous consumption and non-productive investment. Better distribution at the lower level would lead to productivity – raising consumption at that level. The fourth is that the level of living at the base of the income pyramid in South Asia is so 'miserably low' that the suffering makes the effort required by development impossible.

The instrumental value of greater equalization of incomes in South Asia would, therefore, appear to be made out, and the reasons for equality are grounded in that self-interest or prudence which marks the end of ideologies as the incentive to modernization. The independent value of equality remains but its instrumentality is enhanced by removing the ideological element from it.

The third ideology with which Myrdal deals is that of democracy. He discovers the same results from his analysis of democracy in South Asia as he does from that of planning and egalitarianism. Democracy was taken over in the post-independence era directly from the West, and immediately upheld, usually through universal adult suffrage, except in some modified instances. Yet the West had developed its democratic institutions over a long period of time. In these circumstances democracy was adopted and sustained more as an ideology than as a reality in South Asia.

Moreover, when India became independent it was assumed by the political leadership that this would be immediately followed by an economic and social revolution which would be made possible by the institution of democracy in India.

The ideal of political democracy, which practically all the nationalist leaders expounded in their battle against colonialism, is closely related to the ideal of greater social and economic equality. Part of the attraction of the latter was ... the realization that without it political democracy would be an empty achievement. But it was also often regarded as the principal means of carrying out, or of making inevitable, a social and economic revolution.

These twin ideals of revolutionary change in the social and economic condition of the people and the democratic state which would make this possible were, however, not fulfilled. Of the countries in South Asia four of them still have a fairly stable parliamentary government, the others have adopted an authoritarian rule. Where parliamentary government still remains the conditions under which it operates do not lend themselves to the reforms which are necessary. In India the Congress party which started out with high ideals

gradually lost its zeal for reform ... India's failure to make more progress in the direction of welfare democracy reflects the fact that no significant attempts were made to organize the masses, or to impress upon them their stake in agitating for a break-up of the country's rigidly inegalitarian social and economic structure. The impressive façade of parliamentary democracy cannot hide the fact that political participation in any meaningful sense is confined to small upper-class groups ... The political behaviour of the masses is largely controlled by individual personalities who appeal to religious sentiments, caste, or to regional loyalties and antipathies.[24]

In these circumstances the complementary ideology of democratic planning, of which Myrdal makes an extensive study, is an unreality. What it means at best is central planning, the results of which are conveyed to the people through the mass media. Their participation in the creation of the plan, such as happens in France, does not take place.

Explaining the reasons for this, Myrdal says that the fundamental weakness is that democracy in these countries was handed down to them with independence, and unlike western democracies, no struggle or effort was required of the people to win their right to govern. The result has been that the people have not acquired the consciousness of their democratic powers, and they have left it to the upper classes to do the governing for them. In fact, the candidates offered to them at elections have come from these classes.

What is happening as a result of this is twofold. The gilt is wearing off the ideology of democracy and the situation is settling down to greater realism. The other result is that some are looking towards other forms of political organization which will supply them with the social and economic revolution which they need. Among these alternatives is Communism, of which the Chinese version offers attractions to many of the 'educated unemployed'.

The fourth ideology is that of socialism. Again, we have an ideology which has come from the West and been adopted with independence with comparatively few exceptions in the developing countries as the way in which the economic and social life of the people is to be ordered. Frequently it is a vague term, without exact or specific content, to describe a leftist idea. Nehru, in fact, was not in favour of too specific an interpretation:

> Broadly speaking, of course, we know we want a society in which everybody has a rising standard of living, where power is not concentrated and so on and so forth. But the moment you go much further than that – in theory you may – you are trying to imprison your system for the future.[25]

Myrdal thinks that the adoption of socialism by so many developing countries was largely due to the association of socialism with anti-colonialism. Marxism interpreted colonialism as the logical development of capitalism. It was the more eagerly embraced because capitalism took a cruder form in the colonies than elsewhere. He quotes J. S. Furnevall:[26]

> Yet they (the colonial peoples) have, I think, more sympathy with Communist ideals, because they have seen too much of capitalist practice. From economic individualism they instinctively react in the direction of socialism, not necessarily, though not excluding, the textbook socialism of state control over production, distribution and exchange, but of socialism as the reintegration of a society ravaged by unrestricted capitalism – or if you prefer the term – colonialism.

Myrdal's analysis of the application of socialism in Asia leads him to similar conclusions to those reached concerning the other ideologies adopted at the time of independence. Apart from India, state control and ownership of the means of production either was not practised or, if so, it was only temporarily, with the intention of passing it over to private enterprise. Even in India, the socialist principle of state control was only applied in the case of heavy industries which were beyond the capacity of private means to operate. Agriculture, which is the main sector of the economy, remained in private hands. Nevertheless, the ideal of socialism has remained, conveying the ideas associated with it, and giving the people the assurance about the values on which their new life is centred as a hope if not as a fulfilment.

What we seem to be observing, then, is a gradual diminishing of the use and power of ideologies in development. They exercised an important function during the period of nation-building and in mobilizing the masses in the task of modernization. However, a gradual erosion of their mystique has taken place as people have become disillusioned and have been required to look at realities as they are.

Nevertheless, when the ideology arises out of the culture of the people themselves, it continues to be an effective social force. It was in this original way that Nkrumah thought out his philosophy for the building of the state of Ghana through his 'consciencism'. The ideology which he created was designed to appeal to the soul of the African people. Socialism, based on an original African communalism, was its practical expression in social terms. He says:

> I have said an ideology seeks to bring a specific order into the total life of society. To achieve this, it needs to employ a number of instruments. The ideology of a society displays itself in political theory, social theory and moral theory, and uses these as instruments. It establishes a particular range of political, social and moral behaviour, such that unless behaviour of this sort fell

within the established range, it would be incompatible with the ideology.[27]

The power of this ideology exists in its correlation with the African conscience. But, again, look what happened to Nkrumah!

NOTES

1. See *The Dictionary of Philosophy*, ed. D. Runes, Vision Press and P. Owen 1964.

2. For a brief account of this debate see *Study Encounter*, Vol. VI, No. 2, 1970, p. 60, article by Ronald Preston on 'Human Freedom and Fulfilment in a World of Science-based Technology'.

3. Art. cit., pp. 61, 62.

4. See World Conference on Church and Society Official Report, WCC 1967, p. 202.

5. See *Caribbean Integration*, ed. Sybil Lewis and Thomas Matthews, p. 23.

6. Op. cit., pp. 23, 24.

7. See David Easton, *The Political System*, Knopf 1953, and his article on 'Political Science' in *The Encyclopaedia Britannica*.

8. See *The Politics of Development Administration*, Comparative Administration Group, Occasional Paper, pp. 35-8.

9. See Joan Robinson, *The Cultural Revolution in China*, pp. 33ff. which, however, is an idealist picture of modern China, corrected by C. R. Hensman in *China: Yellow Peril? Red Hope?*

10. See *Caribbean Integration*, pp. 21ff. and *Caribbean in Transition*.

11. See *Caribbean in Transition*, p. 15.

12. Second Pan Caribbean Consultation on the work of the Anglican Church with young people, pp. 4ff. Private document.

13. See Aaron Segal, *The Politics of Caribbean Economic Integration*.

14. See E. Haas Stanford, *The Unity of Europe*, 1958, quoted in *The Politics of Caribbean Economic Integration*, p. 2.

15. See *Caribbean Integration*, pp. 21ff.

16. See Gunnar Myrdal, *Asian Drama: An Enquiry into the Poverty of Nations*.

17. See *International Review of Mission*, Vol. LVIII, No. 232, Oct. 1969, pp. 446ff. Review article by Saral K. Chatterji.

18. Op. cit., pp. 711, 712.

19. Op. cit., p. 714.

20. Op. cit., pp. 714, 715.

21. Op. cit., pp. 741-70.

22. Op. cit., p. 767.

23. Op. cit., pp. 745ff.

24. Op. cit., p. 776.

25. Quoted by Myrdal, p. 801, from Nehru's 'Inaugural Speech', Congress Planning Sub-Committee.

26. Op. cit., p. 802.

27. See Kwame Nkrumah, *Consciencism*, p. 59.

9

God and Development - Theology

We have looked at some of the causes of the disillusion of people in the Third World as a result of the failures of the development process. We have seen how their hopes have been disappointed, and we have tried to understand the reasons which they have discovered for the disappointment of their hopes. Neo-colonialism sums up many of the causes which they see. The great political and economic lag accounts for others. Cultural transformation and greater personal awareness, essential prerequisites of modern development, have not yet advanced very far. We have seen what steps are being taken to remedy these defects.

We are left, however, with a feeling that even when these steps have been taken, the disillusion will still remain and that the hopes of the people in the developing countries will not be realized in the form in which they are now entertained. Developed countries have the same experience, of course, of an unrealized hope.

This has caused Christians to reflect on development in the light of their faith. Christian theologians have been asking whether the issues and problems which have been raised by development in the Third World, and indeed by the developed world also, can be illuminated and assisted by trying to understand them in the light of what we believe about ultimate things, by our faith in God, in Christ and in the Holy Spirit, and by what our faith tells us about the world and man. Have some things been left out of development studies which explain the disillusion? Have the ends and the means of development been set in the light of what is true about human nature, human destiny and God's ultimate purpose?

This raises the whole question of theology and reminds us of much that has been said recently about a 'theology of development'. In this penultimate chapter we shall try to see what this demand for a theology of development means, and what help Christians can expect to derive from it in their involvement in development. We do not intend this to be a purely academic exercise. It is meant to help

Christians look at development and their part in it in the light of what they believe so that their actions and their hopes may be realistically informed and they themselves may be sustained by their ultimate hope and faith. It is also meant to help Christians to take another look at what they believe by reflecting upon their experience of development. Our beliefs as distinct from 'the Faith' stand in continual need of information and correction. Development in the Third World is one of those sources from which we can learn much about 'the Faith' and have our beliefs and hopes adjusted to the truth.

In fact, there are three questions which are raised by theology and development and we shall discuss them separately in the remainder of this chapter. The first question is whether and what light does theology throw on development issues? The second is whether and what light does development throw on theology? The third is how do theology and development learn from one another?

The first question whether and what light does theology throw on development was first raised at the Geneva World Conference on Church and Society. The discussion of social, economic and political issues led that conference to feel the need for theological reflection and clarification in order to test in the light of the gospel what they were saying and deciding. It resolved[1] that

Since the conference was not able to discuss adequately its theological orientation, we recommend that the WCC plan a consultation to make a theological evaluation of the conference report, giving special attention to:

(*a*) the measure in which a Christian social ethic can and should make use of notions that are not directly derived from Scripture and tradition;

(*b*) the place of situational and contextual ethics in Christian social thought, and its clarification in the perspective of eschatology;

(*c*) the complementary and dialectical relationship between a rigorous ethic of purity and the ethics of effectivity and compromise, as well as problems posed by both.

Continuing dialogue with natural scientists is needed to clarify the character of man's knowledge of the physical world (nature or creation) and his responsibility in it.

Man's responsibility for the vast increase in technological and scientific power needs to be explored in the light of his own human nature and his stewardship of the grace and plan of God for his creation.

The Christian hope for the renewal of all things in the coming of Christ needs to be continually related, in solidarity with men of political action, to the goals, ambitions, and fears of nations and to international order.

It goes on to ask for theological guidance in revolutionary situations, in the search for national and cultural self-identity in relation to world community, in the effort to create right relations between rich and poor nations, in adopting policies to effect change and in the assessment of the place of ideologies in development and social action.

As a result of this resolution a consultation[2] was held in March 1968 in Zagorsk in the USSR. I do not know of any evaluation of the Zagorsk statement, but its description of itself shows that it recognized that its main concentration had been on social ethics rather than on a theological assessment of Geneva '66. It says:

> Its programme was planned to allow some general theological appraisal of the report ... and in particular to examine more closely the meaning of the 'humanum' as a criterion in ecumenical social ethics.

What Zagorsk did, therefore, was to reflect theologically on the method of Christian social ethics. It outlined the method by which social ethics should be determined. For instance, it emphasized the importance of co-operation with men of other convictions in the process of agreeing on social ethics, the significance of practical consensus among Christians and the need for situation analysis in deciding the course of action which Christians should take. It went on to describe the method by which solutions to controversial public problems should be discovered, expressing a preference for the method of dialectical interaction between the deduction of ethics from given revealed principles and discovering them from experience rather than from either revelation or experience alone.

Zagorsk did, indeed, mark a step forward in theological reflection on social ethics, and it would be a mistake to underestimate the importance of the advance of theological discussion on development issues achieved there.

There is also another advance in this field which Zagorsk was able to make. It was to bring together two departments of the World Council of Churches which have been kept apart from the time they came together to form the Council itself. They are the Department on Church and Society and the Secretariat on Faith and Order. These have been separately organized as if the questions on church and society, which are now mainly those of development, have little or no relation to the theological and ecclesiological issues with which faith and order deals. The consultation at which the theological department discussed the social issues with those whose responsibility it is, marked a step towards the recognition of the unity of theology.

This is a more important move than is often realized. Until recently the church has had to be content with discussing its social issues on the basis of moral consensus alone. It has been assumed that the theological differences between the churches did not offer a basis on which consensus could be reached. This meant the exclusion of theology from the field of developmental and other social problems. Why, it was asked, put the moral consensus to risk by introducing the theological differences which may destroy the possibility of concerted action? Theology's disreputable past was, therefore, a reason for excluding it from the area of the church's concern, and it was assumed that the church could do better without it by relegating it to issues belonging to an area of more remote and less practical concern. Zagorsk marked the beginning of the end of that era. Theology has begun to be reunited with its children.

While we must recognize this important move in the direction of accepting the principle that theology must be heard in development, the limitations of Zagorsk should also be realized. It did not itself attempt a theology of development. All that it was able to accomplish, apart from its statement on social ethics in general, and such problems as revolution in particular, was to think theologically about development through the presence of theologians at the consultation itself. This produced a very important result concerning the method which should be followed in theological discussion of social issues. It was agreed that the method should be christological.

What does this mean for development? It means that in order to understand the issues of development theologically or from the point of view of what Christians ultimately believe about God, man and the world, it is necessary to make Christ himself the criterion of our thinking. In particular we have to understand what the relationship of God and man, in the Incarnation of Christ means. This, in fact, was the approach to the question of reunion which was started at Lund[3] and further developed at the Montreal[4] Conference on Faith and Order. It will be recalled that the older method followed to discover a way to reunion had been a different one. There, it was ecclesiological and, in addition, the comparative method was used. Churches compared their beliefs and traditions with one another in the hope of finding a common denominator through the comparison. On this they hoped that reunion could be based. At Lund, and even more at Montreal, this was set aside and it was decided to start further back with Christ himself and to look at divisions not comparatively but in the light of what christology or the study of the meaning of the Person and work of Christ revealed. Now at

Zagorsk again it was proposed that the christological approach should be adopted in the theological understanding of social issues.

There have been various periods in the debate on the nature of the Church and its unity. The ecumenical conversations first followed the comparative method. It was then discovered that an attempt should be made to start from the central relationship between Christ and the Church and to interpret the differences between the Churches in the light of a renewed understanding of this relationship (Lund method). This method has proved valuable in many respects. Is it not now to be enriched by the consideration of the relationship between Christ and man? The nature of the Church and its unity can be understood afresh only if we begin to understand afresh this double relationship between Christ and the human and Christ and his people.[5]

After Zagorsk the movement to bring theological reflection to bear on the Christian understanding of development gathered considerable momentum, and arrangements were made by SODEPAX to convene a consultation of theologians to consider the question of a theology of development. This was held in Cartigny, Switzerland, in November 1969.[6] The aim of the consultation was 'to attempt to define more closely the methodological problems that arise when theologians look at the process and results of development. It is possible to reflect methodologically upon the manifold theological questions raised by the development problem and this is what Cartigny attempted to do,' says George Dunn in the Foreword.

It would be unwise to try to run ahead of what SODEPAX with its large theological resources is finding will take a long time to conclude. We shall, therefore, do no more than try to interpret some of the consultation papers in the light of our basic problem of the need to help Christians to see development and its issues in the light of their faith.

There is no better point from which to start than the paper presented by Jürgen Moltmann,[7] because he starts from the christological approach, and explains why he does so. His paper is particularly useful, not because we necessarily agree with his theology of hope, but because it illustrates how from the christological approach theology can throw light on development.

Moltmann begins by explaining his christological approach to theological understanding of development. He says there are two other alternative approaches by which the relation of the church and the world have been understood and could be applied to development. They are the classical Catholic model where nature derives its direction and guidance from the realm of grace. This was a meaningful model, he says, when the church was in a position to dominate society. Now that the church has been reduced to a minority status, its ability to direct social change has been diminished and the illusion of the model has been exposed. The church interpreted as the realm of grace is not designed in the divine purpose to rule society from a theological throne.

The other model is the Lutheran idea of the two kingdoms. According to this doctrine, it is by separating the church from the world that the world comes to itself and acquires its authenticity. What happens as a result of Christian faith is that the human reason is liberated from its illusions so as to be itself and to act with complete rationality in secular matters. This liberation, however, says Moltmann, does not actually take place in social terms. It is an illusion of liberation and it is dangerous. Indeed, this illusion of the liberation of the so-called authentic reason is proved by the effects, in social terms, of giving it full expression, 'by their fruits ye shall know them'. You can see that the rationality of the liberated reason is illusory by looking at the structures of society which it has created; and it has killed its own critic.

In place of these two models for understanding the relation of the church and the world, Moltmann proposes another model. It is that of the cross and the resurrection. This model is christological because it is that of Christ who died and was raised to life. He says it is the Christ event which connects the kingdom of God and world history.   *Problem w/ Jesus*

If it is to claim to be Christian, a 'theology of hope and of development' must be grounded in the Christ event itself. It must think of the connecting of God and Man, of the kingdom of God and human history, strictly in reference to this mediator, this connector, to his activity, passion, death and resurrection, and draw the necessary conclusions. In history it is only in the rule of Christ that the eschatological rule of God and with it, the new creation and redeemed existence was mediated. But this rule of Christ is the reconciling and liberating rule of the crucified. How are we to think of this?[8]

He then goes on to show how the 'Christ-event', to use his terms, is the model from which we are to understand the relationship of the church to the world in the development process. He explains that the primary event on which the Christian faith is based is the resurrection. It was from this that the first Christians derived their faith and hope.

Now, they regarded the resurrection of Jesus Christ as the first-fruits of the general resurrection. It was a foretaste or anticipation of 'the final future of history', 'when the whole waiting creation is filled with the peace and justice of a new creation'. It is only an anticipation, though impregnated with ultimate reality. It is a brief model so far as its secular aspect is concerned of what the final consummation will be like. Christ is the representative 'of the coming God', the 'anticipator' of the living new humanity of man in that transformed and redeemed world.

However, says Moltmann, this 'theology of hope' based on the resurrection, has to be seen in the light of the fact that the resurrection happened after Christ passed through the experience of the cross. It is a crucified Christ who is raised from the dead. Moltmann, therefore, goes on to analyse the meaning of the crucifixion. He says it is a sign of Christian experience and involvement in the world. Here he makes one of his most profound observations for development. He avoids the trite moralism that suffering is the price of victory, and says two things that come directly out of New Testament teaching. First, he says that in Christ on the cross we see the victim of the evil in the world. It is through the victim of the sinful secular powers that salvation comes to the world. This is a sign that it is through the victims of modern society that God's future will be born in history.

> If the anticipation of God's future took place in the Christ who was condemned by the law and crucified by the State, this means we are irrevocably shown where in society the anticipations of Christian hope and Christian love are to take place, namely, in those whom Jesus, according to Matthew 25, called the least of his brethren and with whom He identified Himself: 'Visit them and you visit me'. But these do not represent the advanced achievements of society or of economic development but their victims, the hungry, the naked, the homeless, the prisoners, etc.

This resembles the teaching which was so clearly set forward by Bonhoeffer about the meaning of the cross as the sign of the way by which God's help comes to men. For it is through the weakness of God lived by Christ on the cross that redemption comes. The growth and maturation of men is possible only if God limits his own strength; because he is strong enough to impose this weakness on himself.

David Jenkins[9] has something similar to say which relates the same truth to development:

> The power of the powerful is both limited and limiting. On the one hand utopian expectations of a liberation which will overthrow the powers that be and produce a state of liberty where there is no restrictive power and all men are free to enjoy a full life to the full are clearly only dreams. They may be inspiring,

encouraging and creative dreams but there remains the need to give life, meaning and hope to those who, for their lives, will remain part of the powerless and the restricted ... There is at least a tendency in the Bible to make 'the poor' a touchstone of sensitivity and obedience to the will of God. Is this to suggest, as Jesus Christ is the powerless embodiment of the power and love of God confirms, that the creative possibilities of reconciliation and hope ... lie with the powerless, with those who suffer, absorb, love without counting for much or wielding so-called power.

The other thing which Moltmann says about the crucifixion of Christ as a sign of the church's relation to the world, follows directly from what has just been said about the victims of society being the means of redemption. It is that in the crucifixion we see the way in which 'the future of God, of freedom and of justice' are mediated in human history. It is through active identification with those who suffer. It was by identifying himself with men in their sin and suffering that Christ was able to raise them up. It is by living for others and identifying itself with the poor and powerless that whatever mission the church has in human development will be accomplished. 'It is for the sake of those without hope that hope has been given to us.' Speaking about this identification Moltmann says:

> To believers, freedom from law, sin and death is imparted by the power of the Spirit. Already here and now they are prompted by the 'earnest of the Spirit' ... who ... is to be poured out on 'all flesh'. They are not separated from the world, therefore, but stand in, representatively, for the whole waiting creation, as the first fruits of the new creation. In taking up the cross they anticipate the future redemption. In standing in for others, they already live by the future in which justice and life will rule. The community of believers lives by its awareness of others. In this way, it breaks through the law of human society whereby like associates with like. It is made up of 'Jews and Greeks, masters and servants, learned and unlearned, men and women', and only so does it prove that Christ's Spirit lives in it ... In bodily obedience which includes political, social and economic obedience, they follow Christ, and, by doing so, they anticipate here and now, under the conditions of death, the resurrection of the body and of the flesh.

Having laid the christological basis for 'the theology of hope', Moltmann then goes on to draw his conclusions for development. It is here that he makes his unique contribution. In some ways it resembles that of Reubem Alves about whom we shall speak shortly. What he says is that christology offers hope for the future which can be grasped by identification with those who suffer, but it is a future that is open and comes with the release of new powers not envisaged in the technocratic understanding of development.

Moltmann distinguishes here between two senses in which we can speak about the future – the future which 'becomes' and the future which 'comes'. For the future which becomes we have the word *futurum*, and for the future which comes we have the word *avenir*, *Zukunft*, 'happen'. In development philosophy attention has been entirely confined to the future which becomes. That is the future which can be forecast, extrapolated from the forces and powers which are known to exist in the present. In this sense development is merely the evolution or extrapolation of these forces. Futurology thus becomes a science by which the forecasts are made and calculated. Thus you have your 'forecasting units' and your 'look out institutions'. But, says Moltmann, into the planning for the future there should enter not only what is 'calculable' but also what is 'desirable'. Planning which is based only on what is calculable, that is, merely on the basis of technology and unemotional analyses, only serves to hide the actual motives of the dominant forces under the guise of statistics and scientific prescriptions. No account is taken of the future which happens and comes in the way of the New Testament teaching of the Lord who comes.

The basis on which planning of this calculable nature is done is that the future is closed and limited in its possibilities. It is without hope. No imagination is allowed to be exercised on it and in this way the 'calculable' future serves the purposes of those who now hold the power. This is why the student revolution in Paris in May 1968 was a protest against what those, who calculated future possibilities, said was impossible, and the slogan was *L'imagination au pouvoir*.

In summing up his position Moltmann says that for the church the christological conception of the future as open and identification with the powerless poor brings Christians into radical conflict with technocratic views of development.

> The Christian hope in the ultimate future cannot be a party to any higher endorsement or consecration of the hopes inherent in what is now in process of development. That would be a betrayal of the cross and of those whom the Christ called his brethren.

We can see how the values of technocratic development are being questioned and the calculations are being upset by theology.

This is very similar to the position advanced by Reubem Alves[10] which also deserves an extended comment because it shows how theology comments on development. He gives an introductory explanation of the significance of words in theological understanding of society and development. He shows how words, by carrying intelligibility, carry power. They tend to determine policies along the lines of the ideologies hidden within the words. This is why the church has to re-examine its language in the face of great social and cultural change which affects the meaning content of words.

One of the words which Alves examines is 'technology'. This is made up of two words *techne*, which means 'human skill', and *logos* which means 'word' or 'principle of intelligibility'. The compound word 'technology', therefore, means that human skill provides the principle of intelligibility whereby the social order is to be understood. It should be said here, however, that a distinction ought to be maintained between 'technology' which is the science of the application of human skill, and 'technologism' which is its ideological expression and claims to explain facts.

The main presuppositions of 'technologism' are that underdevelopment is an economic problem, and economic problems have to do with quantitative relations and not with qualitative and value questions. It therefore holds that economic analyses and solutions are to be worked out by a highly technical *élite*, and the participation of the people is to be kept at a minimum since this introduces the emotional element which is disfunctional. Man is to be regarded merely as a consumer in the whole process of development.

This 'technologism' is allied to a utopia to which its application leads. 'Utopian technologism' aims at a society which is entirely functional, from which have been eliminated the elements of imagination, creativity and freedom. This functional society marks the utopian end of history for the technologist.

As opposed to 'utopian technologism' Alves advances the idea of 'radical utopianism'. By this expression he seems to mean that the utopia of his choice, and, he would claim, also of Christian choice, is one which is radically different from the static conceptions of technologism.

It involves a change in the idea of utopia, basically as a result of having a radical conception of man. Alves regards man as the creator of the development process. He holds that this conception of man is Christian. It means that he is not simply a consumer, and does not live by bread alone.

He needs to live in a world which makes sense to him, a world filled with human values, a world which is friendly. This is why he makes culture and builds his world: in order to humanize it, so that it will no longer be strange and threatening.

It also involves a change in the idea of utopia because man is considered to be not only the end and purpose of development but also to be 'in process' himself. Man is 'an unfinished product'. This means that man finds his destiny not in a utopia at an end-point in history but in the process of creating a new world. 'Therefore it is amidst the process that man finds his true humanity.'

The radical utopia ... aims at no utopia but at a society which remains permanently open and unfinished. It is a radical utopia because its future is not a day or a place but a permanent horizon, a point of reference which both invites and informs that the task is permanently unfinished.

It is not difficult to see how this theological analysis of technology and man is a very pointed critical comment on development as it is commonly conceived. Modern development philosophy assumes that technology will bring a secular utopia and that this will satisfy men. Alves' analysis shows that this idea of utopia is not theologically sound and this idea of man makes a wrong assumption about his nature. Man is in process and is permanently on the march in a creative activity of making human community. This is why utopia, according to Alves, is radically different from 'utopian technologism'. This is why modern development ideas lead to disillusion.

Moreover, says Alves, 'radical utopianism' is necessary to the creation of a just society and to make possible the changes which are needed in the modern world because it makes the future open. 'Utopian technologism' fixes things. It marks a definite end within history and limits the possibilities of change. It encourages resistance to change by closing the future. Theology, says Alves, exposes this false idea and sets man free to create his own future. The man who sets his heart on the development 'goal' will be disillusioned.

We have taken these two papers to suggest how theology can throw light on development by questioning its assumptions. We do not necessarily agree with the whole position taken up by either Moltmann or Alves, but they help to illustrate the relevance of theology. It might be equally possible, as I would prefer, to use some of the basic christological ideas in St John's gospel and epistles to show where modern development philosophy departs from the Christian understanding of the 'world'. For St John the 'world' has a special meaning. It refers to the state of existence in which people live which lacks the dimension needed to give it fulfilment. Because of this lack, it has the character of vanity and therefore does not carry within itself alone the possibility of fulfilment. It is in relation to this need for fulfilment that St John understands the meaning of the person and mission of Christ. Christ comes from beyond the world as the Son of God. Wherever he is the world is fulfilled. This fulfilment happens as a result of Christ's obedience to the Father, as the Son. Wherever he is following obediently the Father, the creation gets filled with glory. Obedience brings glory when the miracles are performed. Similarly, those who associate themselves with Christ share in this glory when the world, empty in itself, is fulfilled by their obedience. It would not be difficult to translate this into terms of development and to use St John as an effective way to throw theological light on the issues of development. When we look at the disillusion of the developing countries in the light of what St John says about the world, it suggests very strongly the causes of failure and provides a way by which Christians can adjust themselves to the disillusion.

The second question is whether development throws any light on theology. This question has to be understood against the background first, of the need for occasional theological reformulation as a result of changes in thought, language and culture; and second, of the need to re-examine our beliefs continually against the standards of theological truth. Christians inevitably accumulate assumptions and beliefs from their cultural and social situation which need to be constantly examined and corrected. Development experience may be a means of correcting these and an occasion for theological reformulation.

At the Geneva Conference the following conclusion was reached by the Working Group on Theological Issues in Social Ethics:

> It is our conclusion that as a part of its basic task of expressing faithfully in our time the meaning of God's revelation, theology should continue to re-examine its own formulations in the light of dialogue with other disciplines of thought and of the new social experience which Christians share with all men.

Theological reformulation does not mean doctrinal 'revisionism' or change in the basic truths of the faith, as they have been stated in the Catholic creeds. It means stating this theology in a form which is relevant to the thought, language and social context of the time. This exercise in reformulation is not new in the history of the church. Theology has always and necessarily been understood within the cultural and social background of those who have tried to give it expression. When this background has changed new emphases and insights have been acquired. Changes have been made in the way theological truth has been expressed to take account of these new factors.

Indeed, this process is visible within the New Testament itself. Within its pages the interpretation of the Hebrew gospel is already beginning to be expressed in terms of the situation of those who record the events and give instruction and moral advice, both in the gospels and in the epistles. Not only is the gospel being interpreted in terms of the society in which the people live, but also the thought-forms of Greek culture are already replacing Hebrew usages to help people to understand its meaning in their own culture. This process was intensified in the Conciliar period so that the Hebraic culture is almost entirely shed by the theologians of that time. Hellenistic and Latin categories of thought are exclusively used to formulate Christian doctrine. The Renaissance was another period which marked great cultural change. As a result of the new learning the reformation responded to the need for theological reformulation with the great theological activity which marked that period. Today it is development which is creating a situation which demands new theological reflection, clarification and expression based on the original truth of the gospel.

Reformulation becomes necessary, therefore, as a result of change in the social context of life. People's ways of thinking are structured by that context, and when it changes, ideas and ways of thought inherited from the past hinder their attempts to relate their faith to the changed situation. New realities appear in new situations which have a bearing on theological understanding. These have to be accommodated by reformulating and bringing new emphases into theology.

We are able to identify some of these new realities which have appeared as a result of development and have a bearing upon theological insight and so demand reformulation. The first of these is the fact of radical and pervasive change. This tends to destroy those ways of thinking that have favoured a static view of God and have provided divine sanction to institutions in the past. For instance, in the United States in 1850 the most influential theologians in the South were using their theology to defend slavery as a God-given institution. Today their theological arguments have been exploded. The second new reality is the fact that the victims of modern society are more articulate and able to get a hearing for their grievances. They see God as their liberator and appeal to the church to get this liberation implemented. The third reality is the fact that technology has created new forms of communication which have made our world one and interdependent.

As a result of these and other factors interacting with biblical faith we can already see some of the theological agreements appearing. These are outlined by John Bennett in his opening address to the Cartigny Consultation as follows:

First, God is regarded under his dynamic aspect. He is seen to be active in history in the interests of his people. In this respect the way in which God acts in Jesus Christ is adopted as the criterion for discerning his action elsewhere. This means shedding much of the idea of God which removes him from the suffering and struggles of men. God is seen to be involved himself in the human situation without diminishing the responsibility of man for the government of the world.

Second, man is not regarded as either simply a physical being or simply a spiritual being. He is a union of both, so that his physical and spiritual nature interact and influence each other. This lays on the church the responsibility to exercise its mission towards human spiritual well-being in the context of the reality of man's physical nccds.

Third, the church, instead of lending its support unequivocally to the institution of order, though this must not be discarded, must put its emphasis on the claims of the weak, the poor, and the powerless. He quotes Karl Barth:

The Church is witness to the fact that the Son of Man came to seek and save the lost. And this implies that, casting all false impartiality aside, the Church must concentrate first on the lower and lowest levels of society. The poor, the socially and economically weak and threatened will always be the object of its primary concern, and it will always insist on the State's special responsibility for the weaker members of society.[11]

Fourth, there is a growing emphasis on the goodness of the creation. This means that negative attitudes towards the use of the material order have to be re-evaluated in the light of this doctrine and of Christian experience of its implementation in cultural, social and economic terms.

Fifth, there is a general agreement that the church does not exist for itself but for the whole world.

The third question is how can theology and development learn from one another. Here the issue of methodology is raised. The Cartigny Consultation directed its primary attention to the question of the methods by which a theology of development could be created. Its value lies very largely in what it says about methods of theological discourse. The published document contains papers which give the reflections of a few of the participants on the methodology used. Some of these reflections give a useful insight into the issues which lie behind the determination of the method to be used. Conclusions can easily be determined by the methods adopted to reach them.

Paul Löffler[12] gives a careful analysis of the methodology used at Cartigny. After setting out the methods according to types, which he calls 'typological methodology', he then compares the types of methods. This he calls 'comparative methodology'. After which he gives his conclusions on the methods which should be used – 'methodological conclusions'. This analysis is worth study because of the implications of method for theological formulation in the light of development.

It is too early to prescribe what methods should be used, but certain conclusions already stand out. The first is that there must be 'dialectical interaction' between 'the record of faith found in the biblical canon' and 'new insights which have to be checked critically with the experience of the people of God in all ages'. This means that we must not reach our theological conclusions for development straight from the Bible, since the Bible itself did not have development issues in mind when it was written. Nor must they be reached simply from empirical evidence provided by development.

The second is that there must be a plurality of methods used within this dialectical interaction of faith and development experience. Among these we can list the following:

(a) the use in the dialogue of the ethical, pastoral and prophetic insights which are being discovered by Christian communities involved in development;

(b) to compare theological reflections which are being made in different countries and social contexts;

(c) to bring people of other faiths into the dialogue with a view to allowing their insights to comment on both the issues of development and on the theological understanding of Christians.

NOTES

1. See Official Report, pp. 205, 206.
2. See *Study Encounter*, Vol. IV, No. 2, 1968, pp. 70ff.
3. See *The Third World Conference on Faith and Order*, Lund 1952, p. 152.
4. See *The Fourth World Conference on Faith and Order*, Montreal 1963.
5. Art. cit., p. 78.
6. See *In Search of a Theology of Development*, SODEPAX 1970.
7. Op. cit., pp. 93ff.
8. Op. cit., p. 95.
9. Op. cit., pp. 52, 53.
10. Op. cit., Working Paper 16 'Theology and the Liberation of Man', p. 75. Reubem Alves is Professor of Theology at the University of Campinas and Study Secretary of ISAL.
11. Op. cit., pp. 4ff.
12. Op. cit., pp. 26ff.

10

What is Man? - Humanity and Mission

In the previous chapter we considered what light theology throws on development in order to try to explain the disillusion which has been felt about the effects of development, particularly in the developing countries. By placing the experience which these countries have had of development in the light of what Christians believe about ultimate things, we have tried to understand why they have been disillusioned. In this way, through theological reflection, we are beginning to understand better the way in which some of the ultimate realities bear upon development and the factors by which it is conditioned.

One of these is man himself. In fact, man is the main issue. It is out of his mind that the plans for development come. It is with his hands and brains that they are implemented. It is man who benefits and suffers from what happens in the development process. This is the reason why man has become the chief concern of the theology of development. It is important that in whatever the church does in the field of development, therefore, it should have a realistic appreciation of what man is, what his powers and limitations are, and the part which he must play in the process. The church's mission has to take account in the long term of what theology and development are telling one another about man.

It is significant that the World Council of Churches discovered at the time of preparations for the Uppsala Assembly what a remarkable convergence was appearing between the studies being conducted by the several departments and divisions. They all centred on the question of man and the problems which are being raised concerning humanity itself in the development process. As a result a decision was taken at the assembly in 1968 to co-ordinate all these studies under one co-ordinator who would activate and guide them. David Jenkins was in due course appointed to undertake this task. Since that time the results of research and investigations into this subject have been appearing in WCC literature and other publications.[1]

These studies on man have to be understood within the context which gives rise to them. It is the context of development which raises the questions and it is in relation to it that the answers are required. The church has had to face similar issues on other subjects during the last thirty or forty years, and in each case it is the social context which caused the particular subject to be raised. In the 'twenties it was the problem of the person of Christ which was raised by the intellectual ferment caused by liberal theology and historical criticism. The church, therefore, had to face the question of the Jesus of history. In the 'thirties and 'forties when the new ideologies of Fascism and Marxism dominated the scene, the question raised was that of man. This evoked one of the most influential studies of the period in Reinhold Neibuhr's *The Nature and Destiny of Man*. It also decided the agenda for the Lambeth Conference in 1948. It the early 'fifties, when the realities of nuclear fission cast a gloom over secular hopes of a safe world, men's minds turned to the hope of a new world. So attention was directed to the doctrine of the end of the world as it is given in Christian eschatology. At the Evanston Assembly in 1954, therefore, the theme was 'Jesus Christ, the Hope of the World'. By the time of the next assembly the concern of the church had turned to its own problems and, like Vatican II, attention was focused on renewal. While the theme in 1961 was 'Jesus Christ the Light of the World', the attention of the assembly was turned towards the church and renewal and it produced its recommendations on the 'missionary structure of the congregation'.

By today, following on the Geneva Conference on Church and Society in 1966 and the attention given by the Uppsala Assembly to development and the human situation which results from it, the question again is 'Man'. The studies which have been instituted on the question of man are still in the same stage as the attempt to formulate a theology of development. That is, it is not yet clear what is being sought. David Jenkins speaks of a nightmare in which he is faced by a TV interviewer who says 'And what, Mr Jenkins, is all this great new emphasis in the World Council of Churches and its studies about? What on earth is the "humanum"?' 'I suspect,' he says, 'that my answer might go somewhat ,as follows ... On earth it is the latest code word by which people involved in the WCC avoid the question they cannot answer and will not face by raising one more question. None the less, it presents an opportunity and a challenge because it indicates a need. The human study is about men, about us – about us losing our way and finding our way.'[2] Nor is the method by which the search is to be conducted clearly established, though some progress appears to have been made on some methodological issues.[3] It is, therefore, too soon to use the results of these studies in the development debate. All we can do is to indicate the state of the problem and draw upon such studies as have already been made to assist us to understand the issues involved.

One of the most helpful of these studies is provided by Professor Tödt in his address delivered at the Zagorsk Consultation in March 1968 where the theological issues of Church and Society were discussed by the Departments on Faith and Order and on Church and Society. Tödt[4] begins by drawing attention to the meaning of Solomon's prayer for a 'hearing heart'. He says that in the biblical understanding a hearing heart which is open to God's word and God's spirit and allows itself to be called and made by the future is the highest fulfilment of the *humanum*.

Tödt goes on to explain what this means in terms of understanding the essence of human nature. It means that a static definition of man does not do justice to what he is. Man is always being called into the future and he is being created by the response which he makes to that call.

For precisely in the universal upheaval of social systems today we learn that man has not yet found himself, that he does not know who he is and who he will be ... his need drives him to constant changing of the world ... every definition, every determination of the content of the *humanum* violates true humanity, for it establishes man in terms of our present understanding; it reflects only our present situation and, consequently, bars precisely man's openness to the future.

He then goes on to describe how man's problem lies in the fact that he is always creating destructive structures and seems to be continually impelled towards bringing into being situations which deny his peace and fulfilment. Why does man do this? To account for this Tödt makes a quite brilliant analysis of human nature. It is done in terms of the Christian belief in justification by faith, a belief which, we shall see, must continually control the mission of the church in developing countries.

Tödt looks at the *humanum* from three aspects of human experience: activity, suffering and search for identity. That is, he looks at man as an agent of activity, a subject of suffering and a problem of identity. Both in human activity and in suffering, he says, man is in search of his identity and, until he finds himself, both his activity and his suffering, which are essential aspects of his nature, get distorted. Not knowing his true self, what he does and suffers does not attain its end and purpose. This is where the Christian faith comes to his help if he is willing to believe. For the answer to the problem of human identity, of what man is, is offered in Jesus Christ and can be appropriated through faith. Man, as he will be through his response to God's call to him in the open future, where his final nature will be realized, has already been manifested in history in the person of Jesus Christ. Man's activity and suffering, in which he is at present led astray by illusions about his identity, can realize his real nature only in so far as he finds himself by faith in Christ who is the true man. This is briefly what Tödt says.

He illustrates his theme, first by drawing attention to the social and international effects of man's present activity. He describes how and why man is impelled to create destructive structures. Man does have control of the creation. But this control has been diverted into creating structures which are destructive because of man's insecurity and ignorance of what he is. He is driven to aggressiveness. This aggressiveness is born of an attempt to establish his security and so his identity by his own achievements. This aggressiveness has, therefore, come to characterize the activity of *homo faber*. It can be seen in international relations where man builds up his instruments of aggression. These in turn produce counter-aggressive programmes in those against whom he directs his aggression. Tödt illustrates this from modern military technology, and from the counter-aggressive attitudes which are being built up in developing countries against the various forms taken by the aggressive policies of the developed countries. This 'reaggressiveness' in developing countries is indicative of a general situation where destructive structures are inevitable while man acts as he does now in his attempt to establish his own identity by his aggression.

Tödt goes on to say that this insecure aggressiveness is built into man's technological efforts. What he does in the field of technological development mirrors man's effort to establish his identity and his misguided attempts to establish his own righteousness, that is, his identity or personal status. It is man imposing himself on nature. Science and technology reflect the interests of the man himself who handles them. In the structures which he builds up man himself is, therefore, mirrored in all his insecurity and aggressiveness.

Man's problem is clear, if Tödt's analysis is correct. His insecurity is projected into his whole development exercise because he does not know what he is and what he is called to be. He abuses his responsibility and his creative powers in ignorance of what he is. He needs a knowledge of the *humanum* and of what constitutes essential human nature to guide his development programme; 'only a secure knowledge of the *humanum* could provide the criteria to regulate meaningfully the process of active world change'. What, then, is the *humanum*? What is the answer to man's identity?

The same conclusion is reached when we look at the second aspect of human experience and consider man as a subject of suffering. This aspect is a part of human experience at all levels and for all people in some form or other. What Tödt says on this subject is not always quite clear. He says that suffering is to be regarded as an essential part of human experience. Yet it is not to be passively accepted by human society as inevitable in the sense that nothing can be done about it. In so far as it is often caused by human activity it provides an occasion for man to examine the action which causes it and to respond appropriately by remedying it. Having said that, it still remains true that suffering is part of the *humanum*. Indeed, the passion of Jesus Christ, the true Man, makes this clear for Christians.

Two consequences follow from the fact that suffering is a constitutive element of humanity. The first is that it is necessary for man and society to be sensitive to it and to respond to it. This means that we are called to identify ourselves with those who suffer and we are called to attempt to relieve suffering wherever it occurs.

The second consequence of the fact that suffering is a constitutive element of human existence is that it is to be accepted as a means of human development. Unnecessary suffering must be eliminated while at the same time the capacity to suffer must be encouraged and developed. To run away from suffering is to lose the opportunity of becoming truly human. As Tödt says:

> Suffering is a necessary basic structure in the 'humanum', not to be passively accepted, but responded to anew in each situation. One of the greatest tasks which challenge Christianity today is to co-operate in working out the answers for modern man to his fears and sufferings, his pain and frustration; to think them through profoundly and to actualize them concretely. Its origin in the vicarious suffering and death of Christ should continually keep it dedicated to this task; the hope of the resurrection should allow its thoughts to transcend the *status quo* into that dimension where pain and death are no more.[5]

The church is, therefore, able to help man to see a dimension otherwise concealed from him, where his necessary suffering becomes meaningful in that it is a part of 'the *humanum*'. Suffering is part of the experience of the 'true man' who gives men their real identity.

Now both man's activity and man's suffering in development have become problematic. This is because he is unsure of himself. His activity creates development problems for himself and others. His suffering is a mystery to him also because his idea of himself does not allow him to accept this as part of his necessary experience. He does not see where suffering enters into the structure of humanity and, therefore, of the development process. At the same time his powers have increased immensely, even to the extent of being able to change his own physical nature. He does not know what to do. How is he to use these powers in the interests of man? To know this he has to ask the question, what is man? It is the problem of identity. What will remove his insecure aggressiveness and turn it into constructive and creative activity? What will take away his fear of suffering and enable him to accept this necessary experience of humanity as it achieves the stature to which it is called?

This was the question which St Paul faced in his own experience. How could he overcome his own aggressiveness and accept suffering? He says that he had gone about seeking to establish his own righteousness, that is, a status recognized as right, an identity on which he could rely. This had led him further into self-contradiction which he called sin. This struggle continued until he realized that his true self, his righteousness, consisted not in what he had done or was doing. It consisted in what he was going to be by the grace of God and not by his own achievements. His true self has already appeared in the humanity of Christ. Christ accepted him as he was in virtue of what he would become by faith. Knowing, therefore, that his self-realization and the establishment of his identity was something already granted and to be realized in the future by the coming God, St Paul gave up the struggle and abandoned his aggressiveness. He endured suffering as part of his human lot.

> To believe in this situation means to trust finally that God on his own initiative has already accepted man who is futilely striving for his identity and has thus granted him a specific identity. The compulsion to seek his self in action and suffering is dissolved; man finds peace with God (Rom. 5.1). Where Christ lives in man, life acquires the structure of love, of an existence for others.[6]

Man's true identity is to be found in Christ who has come and is to come.

The effect of removing man's essential nature from his past achievements and static nature into the future, is to take away the need for man to justify himself. As his life is not determined by what he has done but by what God promises him in the future, he lives by hope. Anxiety and fear are removed. This has important implications for man's activity and his suffering. His activity can be changed from aggressive self-assertion to love, which sees the other person in terms of his possibilities instead of his past. His suffering is accepted as a necessary experience on the way to the future. Justified by faith, he lives a normal, human life.

Here lies the principle which must guide the action of the church in mission. Just as God justifies man, in spite of all appearances, so the church must demand respect for the humanity of peoples in the developing countries. It means exposing the aggressiveness of those who deny the expression of their responsibility to people in the Third World. It means encouragement when failures occur. It means offering the promise of God's future. It means reducing oneself that others may grow. It means powerlessness that others may have power. It means love.

From these reflections on man as he appears in modern theological debate on development, we now turn to the mission of the church. We shall try to interpret what has been said in terms of what the church should be doing in the developing countries. In doing this I shall be speaking largely out of my own experience of development in Latin America and the Caribbean. The active involvement of the church in these situations provides an opportunity to reflect on academic exercises in development in the light of the actual situation. A great debt is owing to those who have done academic research and study, and it has helped those in the field to understand the factors which determine change and to focus their attention on the right goals. However, in the doing of the development and in the practical involvement, another perspective appears to those who have tried to understand the philosophy and the theology of development. It is from this perspective that I wish to conclude these reflections, and I shall do so by looking at the mission of the church in the situation of development.

These conclusions are also written as an attempt to understand the situation from within the Third World. It would be arrogant to claim that one has perceived what the people themselves, as the local church, feel about the participation of the church in development, and one must speak tentatively. It is a very big mistake for those who are not indigenous to the area to interpret the mind of the people and their feelings. Several have tried this exercise. We shall avoid this here. Nevertheless, some things stand out which are eloquent comments on the mission of the church.

One of these is that we must distinguish carefully between the perspective of the churches of the developed world which have missions in the developing countries from that of the local church. The churches of the developed world tend to project their own problems and solutions on to the developing countries and as a result local policies bear the mark of their influence to an excessive degree. Wherever mechanisms exist through personnel and money to influence local policy, these should be carefully examined with a view to avoiding that influence.

Then, again, a distinction needs to be made within the local church itself between those, on the one hand, who have been colonialized and carry over colonial attitudes and their western orientation into the post-colonial era, and those, on the other hand, who have begun to feel that they must assert their own independence and express their mission in terms of the culture and the needs of the area to which they belong. One of the deepest issues in the Caribbean, as I believe it is in most ex-colonial situations, is to relate these two 'cultures' within the common situation. Some, possibly, tend to underestimate the power and the pervasiveness of, say, English culture in the Caribbean and what it means to the people. For instance, the minority English-speaking groups, who are mainly black, on the east coast of Central America, still feel very sore and deserted because of the new policy of the church to promote Spanish culture in the area. This is an extreme illustration, but one can understand what it means when one is told that in some of the homes of Anglicans in Nicaragua the Queen's portrait is still proudly displayed, and many of them still look towards the Church of British Honduras. 'It is very sad,' said a local resident in Managua to an English visitor, 'that we are no longer Anglican. We have become Episcopalian now.' Nevertheless, the incident illustrates the point that outsiders cannot always distinguish and assess what the people really feel.

This observation has been made by others, particularly in regard to Africa. Bishop Leslie Brown, when he was Archbishop of Uganda, remarked on the difficulty which those who do not belong to the culture of Africa have in understanding the response of Africans to changes in liturgical music. Many clergy arriving in Africa think that the folk-music of the place should be used for worship, but get a negative response from Africans. The reason for this is because this music reminds them of their pre-Christian pagan past and surroundings. This accounts also for the largely negative response to the Missa Luba in the Congo, which was composed by a priest who was not a Congolese. It means that to understand, one must be born in and pass through the experience of the people. This is why observations made by those who think they are 'with' the situation turn out to be more shallow than they realize. In looking at the question of the participation of the church in development in the Third World, therefore, it is necessary to make allowance for the tendency to interpret the facts in the light of a situation and a culture which do not belong to that area.

Having made this qualification we can now look at the basic idea which is raised in the debate about the involvement of the church in development. The question is whether the church should be involved in direct service and action or whether its mission should be to change attitudes of people and direct its attention to those issues which determine the direction in which development goes or is prevented from going. There is a growing tendency nowadays to claim that it is not the church's task to provide the money and other resources for development, but to go to the root causes of the social and economic failures, such as poverty, bad housing and so on, and provoke the right action to be done by those whose responsibility it is. In providing services to alleviate situations of suffering the church has been accused of helping to perpetrate the situations themselves; but unless something is done to change the structures, the church is, in fact, only serving to maintain the *status quo.* This emphasis on the prophetic mission of the church in development over against its service ministry can only be assessed in the actual situation itself. This varies so frequently that policy decisions made about the nature of church involvement by agencies outside the developing countries fail to take account of realities. One frequently meets up with these policy decisions to find that when one tries to apply individual cases to them, the good intentions of those who wish to help are frustrated. It often means that a great deal of money and personnel resources are wasted because the application of a policy is insufficiently flexible to allow for the variations within the situation. Moreover, it leads to accusation of neo-colonial use of resources to impose a policy upon the recipients.

The varieties of situations seem to me to make nonsense of the debate between prophetic and service mission which is seeking to establish a uniform policy. Flexibility is needed. But flexibility demands a particular spirit if it also is not to be abused. Here is where Christians have to relate their action continually to the New Testament and allow it to comment on their action in development. For it is there that the Christian finds his spiritual direction, not simply in the form of rules, but from God's action in Jesus Christ and in God's identification with humanity. In the light of that teaching, development experience tends to reflect two basic spiritual principles.

The first is that all action in development must be motivated by love if it is to achieve its human purpose. Love is an ambiguous word, but reflection on it in the developing world in the light of the New Testament helps to identify its Christian meaning. In development experience we find there are two kinds of love which motivate. One is a selfish love. It gives because giving brings the giver the benefit and not because its primary motive is to help those who receive. Much of the aid that we have looked at in previous chapters is of this kind. It benefits the donor. It builds up his economic empire. It does not help those who receive, not at the point where they really need to be helped, to become equals with the givers. At best it makes them dependent, at worst it destroys their moral being. It is not only money aid which has this effect, but personnel aid also in cases where it takes initiative out of the hands of the local people, where it imposes itself through expertise and other new forms of authority which are calculated to impress and discourage, or else through their magic to fascinate people into inactivity. Experts do this.

The other love is the kind which accepts other people as being equal with and as having the same claims as one has oneself. It recognizes the right of other people to freedom and equality and helps to realize these basic human rights. When love meets another person, that person in a sense becomes yourself. He has a claim upon you which love enables you to recognize and discharge as if it were to your own soul. This love is sensitive to what goes on in the mind of the other person, and if it does not completely understand it is patient and does not impose its will. The moral weaknesses which appear in the other person become a mirror in which one sees oneself, not only as their cause in some way, but also as a partner in guilt. Though by the standards of development the other falls short, love distrusts its own standards and sees new possibilities; in fact, it anticipates them in the other and by giving credit for them makes them real. Yet this love is not paternal and superior, because it knows how empty it is itself apart from the love which it itself is given from outside itself. It is not paternal because it genuinely values and recognizes the other person as better than himself.

Translated into development terms, it is not difficult to see the relevance of this kind of love. But love is two-sided and between equals. It is not the love of the superior for the inferior. Love does not start from the developed country and ooze out towards the poorer nations. Love drops down from heaven upon them both, and neither is superior to the other. In fact, the developed countries are as much in need of love and sensitive understanding as the developing peoples. The developed countries are not God who initiates love. They are human. Their difficulty is that their riches are their poverty and their power is their weakness. They are in great spiritual danger. Here is their underdevelopment. They do not know it. The love relationship of the poor for the rich cannot be expressed in the same way as that of the wealthy for the underprivileged because the poverty of wealth is not fully recognized on either side, nor are the riches of poverty. The developing countries must, therefore, try to learn the proper stance of love.

They have not learned it yet. Nor have they tried. But they must try to learn how to love the powerful. Perhaps it is to stand outside the closed heart and simply wait knowing that here, too, is humanity to be loved – being patient and hoping for them, rejoicing in every sign of humanity which comes from them. Here, indeed, may be the seed of a true relationship – to make each point of contact between the two an opportunity to improve the relationship and grow in love. For love, too, grows and develops.

The second spiritual principle is that all action in development must have as its immediate aim the welfare of humanity. There has been considerable development in recent years. Tremendous strides have been made through science and technology in economic and material or physical development. This, too, can be said of political and social development, but the rate of progress in these areas has not kept pace with that in the physical area. This is frequently given as the reason for human misery in the midst of plenty. This may be true. But unless political and social development is related to what is basically human, human misery will not disappear simply through that kind of development. Humanity must be the goal and end of development. For political and social development does not necessarily make man the criterion. Efficiency, power or security may be the ends. Important though these are, they do not necessarily provide for what is human in man and, in fact, the form of these developments may deny some things which belong essentially to human nature.

The reason why this happens is because the development programme often begins with a wrong conception of what is essential to human nature. Man is not simply a consumer, or an economic gadget, nor is he simply a political animal; neither does psychology describe the total nature of man. The Christian regards man as more than these, and experience confirms this Christian idea that there is something more which belongs to human nature. Essential to human nature is something spiritual for which provision must be made by the social, political and economic context in which he lives. It is this spiritual dimension which lifts man out of his ties to nature and relates him to the future and what is beyond his present limitations. Freedom, moral responsibility, creativity are three expressions of this spiritual dimension which belongs to man. To deny any of them is to harm the human nature of man.

Basic to the other two is freedom, because man cannot be a creator and associate with God in creating a new world if he is not free; neither can he be morally responsible without this freedom. Freedom is, therefore, man's most precious possession, and to love man means primarily to grant him that freedom. That is why the Christian message is all about setting men free and Christ is the great liberator of men. This is why also in the developing countries, particularly in Latin America and the Caribbean, the great demand is for liberation and this is the new word for development in so many of the developing countries of the world. What has characterized the last few years in these areas, more than anything else, is the awakened consciousness of the bonds which are preventing the expression of this freedom, economic, political and social, as well as psychological. Whatever we may say about the excesses to which this demand for liberation goes, it cannot be denied that behind it lies a long and deep frustration of something essential to man's spiritual being which determines his whole life, namely, his freedom.

It is not the excesses to which the liberation movement goes in several areas of human life which alone calls for a Christian critique of it, but the meaning which is attached to it. Liberation must be distinguished from freedom, because to be liberated from the bonds which constrict human activity does not necessarily mean that people have gained that inner freedom which the gospel speaks about. There is a deeper dimension than the external conditions of human life, important though these are to human liberty, which is essential to the *humanum* and being really a man. It is the freedom not only to act and earn a livelihood and live like other people. It is the freedom which enables a man to suffer and to die. It is the freedom that accepts the necessary limitations imposed on man by the realities of social and international life, but does so without constraint. It is a freedom to serve and obey the demands of life without losing integrity. It is a freedom from fear of personal consequences and yet is not rash. It is a freedom from ambition which remains dignified. Where does man get this freedom? That is not the question. The question is, how did he lose it? Because he was created free. Christians believe he lost it through sin and that he has it given back to him eschatologically by identification with the New Man who brings back human freedom and will reveal it fully in the end.

It is in the loss of moral responsibility that lack of freedom manifests itself most in the developing countries. This is particularly seen in those areas where there has been slavery and the loss of civil rights and freedom. The recreation of moral responsibility after the long period of colonial rule is a task which is only equalled or excelled by that of creating this sense for the first time in those societies which have never known the strains of individual and personal freedom until the era of political independence. Moral responsiblity is that inner conviction which belongs to a man that he is accountable for what he does and stands in a direct relationship of duty to someone or something beyond himself in all that he does. This accountability or obligation may appear to be the task or object itself. Christians generally regard it as being owed to God in a direct personal relationship. But there are Christians who identify their obligation with the value of the object which they serve, and quote the parable of the unconscious service done to Christ when it is consciously done to people. In this respect moral responsibility is something which belongs to man, whether he be a Christian or not. This is the sustaining power of service for development. Whether the obligation is owed directly to God or to the object of the service done, it is the only motive which provides a solid emotional basis for development. All other motives seem to turn development sour after the initial stage. This is why development must not only have humanity as its object, but development can only be sustained by what essentially belongs to man, his moral responsibility in freedom to God.

Creativity, along with freedom and moral responsibility, is the third aspect of the *humanum* which is specially relevant to development in the developing countries, and needs to be recognized and built into its programmes. For the Christian it is in this that man shares the image of God who is the creator. Because of it he is called to co-operate in his continual creative work. Creativity means expressing through one's own gifts and abilities and bringing into being what one has conceived in one's own mind. Three elements enter into creative work: the idea, the material and the agent himself. Whenever creative work in this sense is done there is something deeply satisfying and expressive of man's nature, because he is a creator. In the developing countries, however, men have generally been deprived of this total experience. They cease to be creators. They are turned into workers who execute ideas which come from outside. Until provision is made in development for creativity in the full sense, and until indigenous ideas are allowed to be expressed, human frustration will go on. Thus the development process will continue to be deprived of that co-operation which is essential to its success. In this the developing countries share a problem with the developed countries where technology deprives men of creative satisfaction and turns them into tools. The question is, just as freedom can be used as an inner power of restraint, whether creativity can find expression within technology and other situations where man is deprived of primary initiative.

How, then, is all this to be applied in the field itself? How is the practical application of a theology of development and a Christian conception of man to be worked out in detailed policies and programmes? As we have said, it is the spirit in which it is done which finally determines its worth and its effect. But not every spirit is of God and we have to use spiritual discernment in the choice of policies and of the actions which are taken.

Most important of all is the choice of policies which promote human dignity and freedom. The material needs of people have to be provided. But if these are provided in such a way as to continue their condition of dependence, this is not real love. For this reason, the creative and moral nature of all people must be recognized and the help given to them should primarily be to assist them to take responsibility themselves. 'Assist' is not the best word. I should say 'to allow', or even 'to encourage' them to stand on their own feet. This means looking for the right time and the right way to take away the props which hinder their full sense of responsibility. The more responsibility people are given, the more they grow.

It is here that discernment is needed, because in ex-colonial situations, old attitudes built up by dependence tend to encourage us to think that people want to have things done for them. We are inclined to read into developing situations what suits our own selfish kind of charity and to assume that people want decisions to be taken and things to be done on their behalf. Colonial attitudes, which were designed to please those in power, disguise what the people really think. The fact that in committee meetings no opposition is offered to a suggestion made by a foreigner does not mean that it is accepted. Silence is not consent. It often really means that there is no consent, or that they feel that it does not matter what is decided, since those whose opinion is requested cannot implement what they want. Yet, when one is completely open with people about their desire to stand on their own feet, there is no doubt that they want to be able to do without external help and decide things for themselves. The test of love is whether we are willing to help on these terms and not on our own. Is there justification by faith in our charity?

The same question can be asked about decisions made locally. Paternal attitudes are difficult to eradicate, and they are most seen when local decisions are distrusted. It is quite true, of course, that wrong decisions are often made. But they are the price which has to be paid for human growth in responsibility. A man learns more easily by the effect of his decisions than by being told by others that they are wrong or what the right decisions ought to be. Moral responsibility requires that people make decisions, and decision-making must carry with it the power to implement what is decided and responsibility for the consequences. When people know that their destiny is in their own hands and that they are free to decide, they will, possibly after many mistakes, make the right choices in a creative way and carry them out. To doubt this is to fail to apply the doctrine of justification by faith in the developing world.

The same issue arises over the question of indigenization. It is generally agreed that leadership of the churches must pass into the hands of local people. Any other policy would be quite disastrous in the face of the national and cultural self-consciousness which is now promoted everywhere. However sensitive and sympathetic a foreigner may be, he cannot enter into the feelings of the people. The Incarnation itself teaches this, since Christ had to be born a man to become man. No matter how much a man may enter into the life and assimilate the culture of a people, there will always be that gap which birth and upbringing alone can bridge. The best that we can do is to recognize that there are local cultural values. To try to imitate them is really only imitation and, like most imitation, it is laughable. Local people either laugh at it or resent it. Sensitivity means being sensitive to the fact that there is a culture gap. It is because of the importance of cultural affinity and the need to understand situations and people at depth that indigenization is necessary. This means that what by western standards might be considered, but not necessarily are, lower academic and administrative standards is a very small price to pay for local leadership in comparison with the gain in human terms. Again, the doctrine of justification by faith comes to our aid in understanding the importance of indigenization when we have doubts on the subject of human ability and on cultural values.

It is because western values are what they are that indigenization presents some of its most difficult problems. Indigenization should mean not only choosing or making it possible for those to be chosen for leadership who belong to the place; it should also mean that those who take over responsibility do not carry over with them standards and ideas which do not belong to the place. One thinks of the wolves in indigenous clothing. One of the greatest dangers in this respect is for the indigenous ministry to inherit standards and ways of living which cannot be maintained by the local church. This will have disastrous effects on their ministry and provide the wrong motivation for service. Indigenization means more than personnel chosen from the people. It means that they must remain of the people. It means that those who are taking over the mission of the church must not be insulated by patterns inherited from the colonial past from the condition and suffering of their own people.

The triumphalism which the colonial church once enjoyed tends to be inherited by the indigenous church when the circumstances are demanding a new form of mission. With the disappearance of colonialism the time has gone when the church could dictate and dominate the scene and its clergy could claim a position of authority with ways of living appropriate to such a conception of the church. It is the time of the servant church which identifies itself with the

poor and the underprivileged. It is the era of the church which does
not prescribe to the state and to society what it should do. The
church has to live the life of the cross if it is to assist humanity
whose deepest experience is at the level of suffering.

The passing of the triumphalist era of the church means also the
maturity of the secular and the need to recognize the autonomy of
secular disciplines and of the state in particular. The local church,
because of its association with colonial rule, tends to fail in this
regard, and the churches in the developed countries are slow to
respect the autonomy which belongs to independent governments
and churches. In this one detects a failure to appreciate and give
credit for the full human stature of the people themselves in the
developing countries. This means that the church does human
damage where it should be building up humanity in the belief that
every man is born free, morally responsible and creative. Faith in
God's handiwork, which is expressed in trust in the competence of
secular disciplines and authority, is justified in the long run in the
experience of the church in the developing countries.

What has been said, however, has not taken full account of the
negative element in human nature. Man's sin and selfishness introduce factors into development which our emphasis on freedom,
responsibility and creativity tend to obscure. The autonomy of the
secular must be considered alongside the fact that it is often used
to serve the less worthy aspirations of men. Within the social complex man is divided into competing individuals and groups with
their own selfish aims. As long as these sinful forces are allowed
to express themselves and are not brought under control, and
as long as people and groups stand in contradiction and opposition
to one another, without seeing the consequences of their attitudes
and actions, the emphasis which we have laid on creativity will be
used in the service of personal and group greed. Freedom will be
turned into licence.

Of all the institutions designed to deal with the human situation,
the church is the best equipped to understand the meaning of sin
and, therefore, has a positive mission in developing countries to
help people to deal with it. The church knows from its gospel that
the first effect of sin is to create divisions between persons and that,
therefore, the meaning of the mission of Christ has to be understood
largely in terms of reconciliation. It is this work of reconciliation
which seems to be the primary task of the church in the field of
development. It has a prophetic task too, but my own experience
tends to emphasize the need of reconciliation. The church is called,
I think, to reconcile, to open up avenues of communication between
persons, groups and sectional interests.

Richard Dickinson, the author of *Line and Plummet*, and one of the most profound thinkers on development issues, has drawn attention lately[7] to some of the chief faults in development programmes. He has identified them as arising out of a failure to bring separate sectional and group interests into a common understanding and effort. He therefore regards it as the primary mission of the church to bring these interests together. He says that projects undertaken by the church should have a 'relationship orientation', that is, they should be so programmed that they take account of the need to bring people into co-operative effort and understand one another's interests. The mission of the church in development is reconciliation. It is not its task to tell people how to perform their job, nor is the church competent to do it for them. It should encourage people in the struggle by reminding them of the endless possibilities of human development, and persuade them to forgive one another so that they will work harmoniously together in the interests of the happiness which is God's purpose for man.

NOTES

1. See David Jenkins, *What is Man? Technology and Social Justice* ed. R. H. Preston, and articles in *Study Encounter*, etc.

2. See *Study Encounter*, Vol. V, No. 4, 1969, p. 159, article by David Jenkins, 'Towards a Purposeful Study of Man'.

3. Art. cit., pp. 151ff.

4. See *Study Encounter*, Vol. IV, No. 3, 1968, article 'The Christian Understanding of Man in view of the Questions raised by Changes in Modern Society'.

5 Art. cit., p. 119.

6. Art. cit., p. 120.

7. See *The Ecumenical Review*, Vol. XXII, No. 3, July 1970, 'Toward a New Focus for Churches' Development Projects', and *International Review of Mission*, Vol. LVIII, No. 232, Oct. 1969, 'Church-Sponsored Development Efforts'.

Bibliography

General

Abrecht, Paul, *The Churches and Rapid Social Change*, SCM Press 1961.
Almond, G. A. and Coleman, J. S., *The Politics of Developing Areas*, OUP 1960.
Alves, Reubem, *A Theology of Human Hope*, Corpus Books, Washington 1969.
Audic, F. M. and Matthews, T. G. (eds), *The Caribbean in Transition: Papers on Social, Political and Economic Development*, Institute of Caribbean Studies, University of Puerto Rico 1965.
Baranson, J., *Technology for Underdeveloped Areas* – An Annotated Bibliography, Pergamon Press 1967.
Bauer, G., *Towards a Theology of Development*. An Annotated Bibliography, SODEPAX 1970.
Bennett, John C. (ed.), *Christian Social Ethics in a Changing World*, SCM Press and Association Press 1966.
— *Foreign Policy in Christian Perspective*, Scribners, NY 1966.
Black, C. E., *The Dynamics of Modernization*, Harper & Row, NY 1966.
Brode, John, *The Process of Modernization*. Annotated Bibliography on the Sociocultural Aspects of Development, OUP 1969. .
Camera, Helder, *Church and Colonialism*, Sheed & Ward 1969.
Cesaire, Aimé, *Discours sur le Colonialisme*, Présence Africaine, Paris 1955.
Cooley, Frank, *Indonesia – Church and Society*, Friendship Press, NY 1968.
Cragg, Kenneth, *Christianity in World Perspective*, Oxford Univ. Press 1968.
Devandan, P. D. and Thomas, M. M., *The Gospel and Renascent Hinduism*, WCC 1959.
— *Christian Participation in Nation Building*, WCC 1960.
Dickinson, Richard, *Line and Plummet*, WCC 1968.
Drucker, P., *The Age of Discontinuity*, Harper & Row 1969.
Elliott, Charles, *The Development Debate*, SCM Press 1971.
Ellul, Jacques, *Politique de Dieu, politique de l'homme*, Ed. Universitaires, Paris 1966.
Fanon, Frantz, *Towards the African Revolution*, Harmondsworth : Penguin Books, 1968.
— *The Wretched of the Earth*, MacGibbon & Kee 1965 and Penguin Books 1966.
First, Ruth, *The Barrel of a Gun*, Allen Lane The Penguin Press 1970.
Friere, Paulo, *La educación como practica de la libertad*, Montevideo, Tierra Nueva.
— *Pedagogy of the Oppressed*, Herder & Herder, NY 1968.
Galbraith, J. K., *The Affluent Society*, Houghton Mifflin Company 1969.
— *The New Industrial State*, Houghton Mifflin Company 1967, 1971.

Gandhi, Mahatma, *An Autobiography*, Cape 1966.

Hamid, Idris, *In Search of New Perspectives*, CADEC, Box 616, Barbados, West Indies.

Hensman, C. R., *China: Yellow Peril? Red Hope?*, Westminster Press 1969.

Jarrett-Kerr, M., *Christ and the New Nations*, Morehouse-Barlow 1966.

Jenkins, David E., *The Glory of Man*, SCM Press 1967.

— *What is Man?*, Judson Press 1971.

Johnson, Byron L., *Need is Our Neighbour*, Friendship Press, NY 1966.

Kaunda, Kenneth, *A Humanist in Africa*, Longmans 1966.

Kraemer, Hendrick, *World Cultures and World Religions*, Lutterworth Press 1960.

Lee, R. and Marty, M. E. (eds), *Religion and Social Conflict*, OUP, NY 1964.

Leeuwen, A. T. van, *Prophecy in a Technocratic Era*, Scribners, NY 1968.

— *Christianity in World History*, Edinburgh House Press 1964.

Lewis, Sybil and Matthews, Thomas (eds), *Caribbean Integration: Papers on Social, Political and Economic Integration*, Institute of Caribbean Studies, University of Puerto Rico 1967.

Lewis, W. A., *The Theory of Economic Growth*, Harper & Row 1970.

Little, I. M. D., *Aid to Africa*, Pergamon Press 1964.

— and Clifford, *International Aid*, Allen & Unwin 1965.

Mannheim, Karl, *Essays on the Sociology of Culture*, Routledge & Kegan Paul 1967.

Marcuse, Herbert, *One Dimensional Man*, Beacon Press 1964.

Matthews, Z. K. (ed.), *Responsible Government in a Revolutionary Age*, SCM Press and Association Press 1966.

Mboya, Tom, *Freedom and After*, Little, Brown and Company 1963.

Mead, Margaret, *Cultural Patterns and Technical Change*, A Mentor Book, New American Library and UNESCO 1965.

Mosley, J. B., *Christians in the Technical and Social Revolutions of Our Time*, Forward Movement Publication, NY 1966.

Moyes, A. and Hayter, T., *World III Developing Countries*, Pergamon Press 1964.

Munby, Denys (ed.), *Economic Growth in World Perspective*, SCM Press and Association Press 1966.

— *God and the Rich Society*, OUP 1961.

— *Christianity and Economic Problems*, Macmillan 1956.

Myint, H., *The Economics of the Developing Countries*, Praeger 1965.

Myrdal, Gunnar, *Asian Drama: An Inquiry into the Poverty of Nations*, 3 vols, Penguin Books 1968.

Newbigin, Lesslie, *Honest Religion for Secular Man*, Westminster 1966.

Nkrumah, Kwame, *Africa Must Unite*, International Publishers Co. 1970.

— *Consciencism*, Heinemann 1964.

Nolde, O. F., *Free and Equal*, Human Rights in Ecumenical Perspective, WCC 1968.

Preston, R. H. (ed.), *Technology and Social Justice*. A symposium sponsored by the International Humanum Foundation. Judson Press 1971.

Robinson, Joan, *The Cultural Revolution in China*, Penguin Books 1969.

Schram, Stuart, *Mao Tse-Tung*, Penguin Books 1966.

Segal, Aaron, *The Politics of Caribbean Economic Integration*, Institute of Caribbean Studies, University of Puerto Rico 1968.

Shaull, Richard, *The New Revolutionary Mood in Latin America*, NCC, USA, NY 1962.

Sinai, I. R., *The Challenge of Modernization*, Norton, NY 1964.

Smith, D. Eugene, *India as a Secular State*, OUP 1963.
Snow, Edgar, *Red Star over China*, Grove Press, Inc. 1968.
Taylor, John, *The Primal Vision*, SCM Press 1963.
Thomas, M. M., *The Christian Response to the Asian Revolution*, SCM Press 1966.
Tinbergen, Jan, *Shaping the World Economy*, Twentieth Century Fund, NY 1962.
— *Development Planning*, Weidenfeld & Nicolson 1967.
U Thant, *United Nations Development Decade at Midpoint*, UN 1965.
Vaughan, B. N. Y., *Structures for Renewal*, Alec R. Allenson, Inc. 1967.
— *Wealth, Peace and Godliness*, Alec R. Allenson, Inc. 1968.
de Vries, Egbert, *Man in Rapid Social Change*, SCM Press 1961.
— (ed.) *Man in Community*, SCM Press and Association Press 1966.
Ward, Barbara, *The Rich Nations and the Poor Nations*, W. W. Norton and Company, Inc. 1962.
Weber, Hans-Ruedi, *Asia and the Ecumenical Movement*, Allenson 1966.
Whiteley, D. E. H. and Martin, R., *Sociology, Theology and Conflict*, Blackwells 1969.
Wish, J. R., *Economic Development in Latin America*. An Annotated Bibliography, Pall Mall Press-Praeger, NY 1966.

Reports and Studies

BRITISH COUNCIL OF CHURCHES

World Poverty and British Responsibility, SCM Press 1966.

WORLD COUNCIL OF CHURCHES (GENEVA)

General Assembly Reports

The Evanston Report. Second Assembly of the World Council of Churches, 1954, SCM Press 1955.
The New Delhi Report. Third Assembly of the World Council of Churches, 1961, SCM Press 1962.
The Uppsala Report. Fourth Assembly of the World Council of Churches, 1968, WCC 1968.

Faith and Order Reports

The Third World Conference on Faith and Order, Lund 1952, ed. Oliver S. Tomkins, SCM Press 1953.
The Fourth World Conference on Faith and Order, Montreal 1963, ed. P. C. Rodger and L. Vischer, SCM Press 1964.
Faith and Order Findings. Report to the Fourth World Conference on Faith and Order, ed. Paul S. Minear, SCM Press 1963.

Church and Society Reports

The Common Christian Responsibility Towards Areas of Rapid Social Change. Second statement, WCC 1956.
WCC Project Papers on Rapid Social Change:
Philip, André, *Europe and the Underdeveloped Countries* (3);

Neibuhr, Reinhold, *The International Class Struggle* (9);
Bilheimer, R. S., *Ethical Problems of Economic Aid and Technical Assistance*;
Steltzer, Th., *The West and the Areas of Rapid Social Change* (11);
Metzer, J. D., *Hunger. A Challenge to the Church Today* (19).
Dilemmas and Opportunities: Christian Action in Rapid Social Change. Report of an International Ecumenical Study Conference, Thessalonika 1959, WCC 1959.
World Conference on Church and Society, Geneva 1966. Christians in the Technical and Social Revolutions of our Time. The Official Report by M. M. Thomas and Paul Abrecht, WCC 1967.
Preparatory Studies for this Conference, SCM Press and Association Press 1966:
Christian Social Ethics in a Changing World ed. John C. Bennett;
Economic Growth in World Perspective ed. Denys Munby;
Man in Community ed. Egbert de Vries;
Responsible Government in a Revolutionary Age ed. Z. K. Matthews.

Other Reports and Statements

The Arnoldshain Report 1956. A Regional Conference on the Responsible Society in National and International Affairs, WCC 1956.
Conflict, Violence and Peace ed. A. M. Barkot, WCC 1970.
Development Education. Report of a Consultation sponsored by the Secretariat on Development Education, WCC 1969.
Experiments with Man ed. Hans-Ruedi Weber. Report of an Ecumenical Consultation, WCC 1969.
Leisure Tourism – Threat or Promise. Report of a Consultation held autumn 1969, WCC 1970.
Uppsala Speaks ed. Norman Goodall, incorporating Message and Section Reports, WCC 1968.

SODEPAX

World Development: Challenge to the Churches, Beirut Conference, 1968.
The Challenge of Development, Montreal Conference, 1969.
Peace – The Desperate Imperative, Baden Consultation, 1970.
Partnership or Privilege?; An Ecumenical Reaction to the Second Development Decade, 1970.
In Search of a Theology of Development. Papers from a Consultation on Theology and Development held in Cartigny, 1970.
Towards a Theology of Development. An Annotated Bibliography prepared for SODEPAX, 1970.
The Plenary Meeting, June 21-27 1970 (The Nemi Report).
Money in a Village World: The Interests of the Developing Countries and International Monetary Reform, 1970.

UNITED NATIONS (NEW YORK)

The United Nations Development Decade – Proposals for Action, UN 1962.
Towards a New Trade Policy for Development. Report of the Secretary General of UNCTAD, 1964.

Development Assistance: Efforts and Policies, OECD 1965.

1965 Report on the Social Situation with Special Reference to Popular Participation and Motivation for Development, UN 1966.

United Nations Conference on Trade and Development – Second Session (New Delhi), Vol. 1, Reports and Appendices, 1968.

The Indicative World Plan for Agricultural Development, FAO 1969.

Partners in Development. Report of the Commission on International Development (Pearson Report), Pall Mall Press and Praeger, NY 1969.

Towards Accelerated Development. Proposals for the Second UN Development Decade (Tinbergen Report), UN 1970.

AFRICA

Drumbeats from Kampala. Report of First Assembly of All-African Conference of Churches, Kampala, Africa, WCC 1963.

Church in Changing Africa. Report of the All-Africa Church Conference, Ibadan, Nigeria, WCC 1958.

Africa in Transition – The Challenge and The Christian Response, WCC 1962.

Africa Surveys I and II, Report by Z. K. Matthews and Sir Hugh Foot, WCC 1964/65.

EAST ASIA CHRISTIAN CONFERENCE

The Christian Prospect in Eastern Asia – Papers and Minutes of the Eastern Asia Christian Conference, Bangkok, 1950.

The Common Evangelistic Task of the Churches in East Asia – Papers and Minutes of EACC held in Prapat, WCC 1957.

To Understand Christian Responsibility in the Asian Industrial Awakening. Report of First East Asia Conference on Industrial Evangelism, Manila, 1958, EACC and WCC.

Witnesses Together, Report of EACC, Kuala Lumpur, 1959, ed. U. Kyaw Than.

One People, One Mission, ed. J. R. Fleming, WCC 1963.

EACC Assembly Minutes, Part I, Bangkok 1964. Part II, The Christian Community Within the Human Community 1964.

Liberation, Justice, Development, Workshop Reports and Recommendations from the Asian Ecumenical Conference for Development, Tokyo 1970, WCC 1970.

LATIN AMERICA

Christians and Social Change in Latin America – Findings of First Latin American Evangelical Consultation on Church and Society, Peru, WCC 1961.

Second Consultation held at El Tabo, Chile, 1966. See Background Information, World Council Occasional Publication, 1966.

Conclusiones de la Tercera Conferencia Evangelica Latinamericana, in Criterio XLII, 1580 (Sept. 25, 1969) 659-663. An evangelical consultation.

Statements and Declarations

The Charter of Algièrs – Statement by Developing Countries, 1968.
The Hazlemere Declaration, published by the Hazlemere Declaration Group, 515 Liverpool Road, London, N.7 1969.

Declarations by Roman Catholic Priests

Carta de un grupo de sacerdotes en Chile, CIDOC, Cuaderno, No. 10, Vol. 5
Declaracion de Sacerdotes Peruanos, CIDOC, Cuaderno, No. 21, Vol. 7 (1968), 91/1-7 reprint.
(1968), 39/1-12 reprint.
Il Encuentro del grupo sacerdotal de Colconda (The Colconda group) in *Cristianismo y Sociedad* 7, 19, 39-50.
See *Concilium*, Vol. 3 V (1969) 62-71, for assessment of attitude of priests towards revolution.

Papal Statements

John XXIII   *Mater et Magistra*.
John XXIII   *Pacem in Terris*.
Vatican II   *Gaudium et Spes*.
Vatican II   *Dignitatis Vitae*.
Paul VI   *Populorum Progressio*.
Paul VI   *Humanae Vitae*.

Célam

'Presencia Activa de la Iglesia en el desarollo y en la integracion de America Latina', in *CIAS* XVI, 167 (Oct. 1967) 21-35.
'La Iglesia en la actual transformacion de America Latina a la luz del Concilio Vaticano II', in *Criterio* XLI, 1558 (Oct. 24, 1968) 757-804, The Medellin Document.
'Manifesto de las Obispos del Tercer Mundo', in *CIAS* XVI, 169 (Dec. 1967) 21-29. Comment by Latin American Bishops on *Populorum Progressio* and obligations of priests.

Periodicals

The Ecumenical Review, WCC

Vol. XVIII, No. 4, Oct. 1966.

Thomas, M. M., 'Modernization of Traditional Societies and the Struggle for a New Cultural Ethos'.
Wendland, H., 'The Church and Revolution'.
Borovoy, V., 'The Challenge and Relevance of Theology to the Social Revolutions of our Time'.
Blake, Carson, 'How the Church contributes to the Transformation of Society'.
Schiotz, F. A., 'Theological Guidelines for the Church's Involvement in International Affairs'.

Vol. XIX, No. 2, April 1967.

Articles for the Twentieth Anniversary of the Commission of the Churches on International Affairs.

Vol. XX, No. 3, July 1968.

Kohnstamm, Max, 'Some Remarks about Structuring International Effort'.
Ward, Barbara, 'Action for the Future'.
Chronicle includes 'Imperatives of Peace and Responsibilities of Power' and 'Statement of the Beirut Conference on World Co-operation for Development'.

Vol. XX, No. 4, Oct. 1968.

contains: Addresses at Fourth Assembly, Uppsala, 1969.

Vol. XXI, No. 3, July 1969.

Rossel, Jacques, 'From a Theology of Crisis to a Theology of Revolution. Karl Barth, Mission and Missions'.
Booth, Alan, 'Imperialism, Economic Development, and the Christian World Mission'.

Vol. XXI, No. 4, Oct. 1969.

Berkhof, H., 'Reopening the Dialogue with the Horizontalists'.
Chronicle includes 'An Ecumenical Programme to Combat Racism' (Approved at Canterbury by WCC Central Committee).

Vol. XXII, No. 1, Jan. 1970.

Alves, Reubem, 'Protestantism in Latin America. Its Ideological Function and Utopian Possibilities'.

Vol. XXII, No. 3, July 1970.

Dickinson, R., 'Toward a New Focus for Churches' Development Projects'.
Fernandez, Angelo, 'The Role of the Church in Development'.
Chronicle includes 'Manifesto to the Nation' (Bolivia).

Vol. XXII, No. 4, Oct. 1970.

Jenkins, David, 'The Bearing of Chalcedon upon the Modern Discussions about the Humanum and the Secular'.

International Review of Mission, WCC

Vol. LVIII, No. 232, Oct. 1969.

Cragg, K., 'The Tempter Said. Reflections on Christian Theology and Development'.
Nagy, G., 'The Church and the Aims of World Development'.
Land, P., '*Populorum Progressio*. Mission and Development'.
Fernando, E., 'Integral Development – Reflections of a Conservative Evangelical from a Developing Country'.
Dickinson, R., 'Church-Sponsored Development Efforts'.
Zulu, J. B., 'The Goals of Development as seen from an African Humanist Perspective'.
Davidson, G. W., 'Myths of Identity: Factors in Development'.
Review Articles on *Asian Drama*, etc.

Vol. LIX, No. 234, April 1970.

Barkat, A. M., 'The Quests of Contemporary Asia'.
Fonseca, A., 'Challenges of Asian Development'.
Park, S. J., 'The Role of Youth in Asia Today'.

Vol. LIX, No. 235, July 1970.

George, P. J., 'Racist Assumptions of the 19th Century Missionary Movement'.
Deschner, J., 'Ecclesiological Aspects of the Race Problem'.
Anderson, J. F., 'A Time to Heal. A Southern Church deals with Racism'.
Fitzpatrick, J. P., 'Faith, Freedom and Cultural Difference: Cuernavaca and Christian Mission'.

Study Encounter, WCC

Vol. II, No. 1, 1966.

Mead, Margaret, 'The Quest for the Truly Human'.
Hoch, E. M., 'The Healing Community'.
Fagley, R. M., 'The Struggle for World Community'. Report.

Vol. III, No. 1, 1967.

Smythe, D. W., 'The Political and Economic Condition of Freedom of Information'.

Vol. IV, No. 2, 1968.

'Theological Issues of Church and Society – Statement of the Zagorsk Consultation.'

Vol. IV, No. 3, 1968.

Tödt, H. E., 'The Christian Understanding of Man in view of the Questions raised by Changes in Modern Society'.
Co-ordinated Studies on Man (the *humanum* in a Changing World).
Report on the Future of Ecumenical Study and on the co-ordinated studies on Man.
Gruber, Pamela, 'Conference on World Co-operation for Development', World Council of Churches and UNIAPAC Joint Conference.

Vol. V, No. 1, 1969.

Verghese, Paul, 'Humanization as a World Problem'.
MacKoy, D. M., 'Information Technology and the Manipulability of Man'.

Vol. V, No. 2, 1969.

Kohnstamm, Max, 'Problems involved in Building a World Community'.
Elliott, Charles, 'Growth, Development ... or Independence?'.

Vol. V, No. 4, 1969.

Jenkins, David E., 'Towards a Purposeful Study of Man'.

Vol. VI, No. 2, 1970.

Abrecht, Paul, 'The Ecumenical Obligation to think about the Future of Man and Society in the Light of the Technological Revolution'.
Preston, Ronald, 'Human Freedom and Fulfilment in a World of Science-Based Technology'.
Gill, David M., 'Power, Violence, Non-Violence and Social Change'.
Streetam, Paul, 'Enoch Powell, the Churches and Aid'.

INDEX

Africa, 49, 51, 52, 55, 57, 61, 67, 69,
    72, 73, 90, 91, 97, 98, 106, 110,
    123, 124, 129, 162
    South, 41
    Southern, 43
Afro-Asian Conference, Bandung
    (1955), 5, 48, 50, 51
Agriculture, 73, 138
Ahiram, E., 24
Aid, 69-73, 164
    plan, 73
    target, 16
Alves, Reubem, 148, 149, 150
Allende, President, 35
Algiers, Charter of, 2
Anderson, Professor Robert, 122, 129
Andic, Fuat M., 24
Andriamanjato, Richard, 49, 52
Asia, 61, 69, 102, 113, 114, 130, 132,
    135, 136

Bâle Agreement, 30
Bank of International Settlements, 30
Barth, Karl, 153
Bennett, John, 152
Black, C. E., 96
Burgelin, Henri, 55
Braithwaite, Professor, 126
British Honduras, 55, 73, 78, 162
Buddhism, 10, 87, 91

Caio de Toledo, 1
Carribbean, 22, 24, 51, 53, 58, 85, 91,
    125, 126, 127, 128, 129, 161, 162,
    166
    Free Trade Association, 28
Central American Common Market,
    28
Cesaire, Aimé, 49
Change,
    causes, 5, 32
    economic, 5, 32
    effects,
        cultural, 4-5
        moral, 4
        psychological, 4
        social, 4

structural, 25-28, 33
China, 38, 62, 69, 77, 88, 92, 98, 103,
    106, 125, 137
Christ, 143-148, 159, 160, 163, 169,
    170
    cross and resurrection, 145-147,
    170
Christianity, 9-10, 17, 63, 72-73, 99,
    120
    reformulation, 151-152
    theology of development, 10, 46,
    140, 150, 154
    theology of hope, 144-148
Church, 17, 37, 66, 144-145, 148,
    153, 161, 169-171
    attitude towards violence, 40-47
    crisis in action, 10
    crisis in theology, 10
    mission, 161, 163, 171
    role in development, 47
Church and Society in Latin
    America (ISAL), 34
    Piriapolis, 34
Creativity, 167
Colonialism, 48
    criticism of, 49, 52
    cultural effects, 51
Conteris, H. B., 120
Craig, Albert M., 88
Culture, 8, 9, 86, 87, 93, 95, 110, 162
    definition, 78
Cybernetics, 94-95

Demas, William, 22
Devanandan, P. D., 63
Development,
    an illusion, 1-12
    church action, 12
    Decade, 1, 14-15
    desarrollismo, 35
    not solely economic, 18-19
    planning, 131
    poverty gap, 3, 23
    purpose, 3-4
    relationship with donor, 19-22, 26
Dickinson, Richard, 170
Dunn, George, 144